Kays Gary,
Columnist

Kays Gary, Columnist

A collection of his writings
compiled by his friends

Edited with a foreword by
C. A. McKnight

The
East Woods
Press

Library of Congress Cataloging in Publication Data

Gary, Kays, 1920-
    Kays Gary, columnist.

    Columns originally published in the Charlotte
Observer.
    I. McKnight, C. A. II. Observer (Charlotte, N.C.)
III. Title.
AC8.G34   081   81-68572
ISBN 0-914788-43-4   AACR2

The columns and photographs in this book first appeared
in The Charlotte Observer and are reprinted here with
permission.
Cover illustration by Gene Payne.
Typography by Raven Type.
Printed in the United States of America.

An East Woods Press Book
Fast & McMillan Publishers, Inc.
820 East Boulevard
Charlotte, N.C. 28203

Publisher's Note

In producing this book, I have had to call upon the services of an unusual number of people who willingly and cheerfully gave their time and skills in order to help honor a man who has always been ready to assist a human being in need.

I would like to thank Pete McKnight for his wisdom in conceptualizing this book and his hard work during a time when he really deserved a rest. A very special thanks to the indefatigable Dot Jackson, for haunting the tombs of The Observer and bringing back treasures from Kays Gary's earliest columns, and for always making the selection process fun ("Heeee! Listen to this ol' rascal . . ."). Thanks also to Ed Williams and Jack Claiborne for their help with the final culling down, which is always the most difficult task.

A special thank-you to Gene Payne, who drew a studied portrait of Kays Gary for the jacket of this book, and to Eddie Owens, who helped Dot Jackson hunt down old columns.

Thanks to all the people, too numerous to recall here, who wrote in with reminiscences and tributes to Kays Gary. Included in this long list are faithful readers who have been waiting for years for such a book to come into print, many of whom sent us a favorite column or two that now appear in this book. Some of the brief tributes are printed in this book or on its jacket, and we owe the writers a grateful acknowledgment for adding to the profile of Kays Gary.

Warm gratitude is also felt for Rolfe Neill, publisher, and Rich Oppel, editor, The Charlotte Observer, for their continued support and for permission to reprint the columns and photographs in this book.

I suppose in my list of acknowledgments I would be overlooking the obvious if I did not take a few words to thank Kays Gary. During this whole project, Kays kept apologizing for not being more helpful. He could not get it into his head that this book was intended to be a celebration of him, not a collection compiled by him. Of course, I must confess that one reason for this is that, had we assumed the latter course, the book simply would never have made it to the printer. The few times Kays did work with us, he would bend our ears for hours about all the little details surrounding a story that never got into print. At his rate, this book would have been another twenty-five years in the making! But, I digress. . . . Thank you, Kays Gary, for being the fine spinner of true tales that you are.

Sally Hill McMillan
Fast & McMillan Publishers, Inc.

Kays Gary, Columnist

Contents

Foreword

Kays Gary has been a Charlotte Observer columnist since 1956. Before that, he was a reporter and feature writer and a very good one, too. Early that year we entered some of his stories in the national Ernie Pyle contest, named for the famed World War II reporter/columnist who told the folks back home what it was really like to be in the deserts of Africa or landing on the beaches of the South Pacific. Gary won first place, went to Washington to receive the award, and came home with a check for $1,000, quite a bonus for a young man who had been hired off The Shelby Daily Star for $95 a week just four years earlier by the late Ernest B. Hunter, Observer managing editor.

Gary gives me credit for suggesting that he start a three-times-a-week personal column after winning the Ernie Pyle award. If that is true, I take it as a dubious compliment. In his reporting for The Observer, especially his stories about people, Gary had already displayed the sensitivity and his own way with words that were to capture and hold the interest of readers of all ages in all parts of the Piedmont where The Observer circulates. I should have seen his potential as a columnist much earlier.

We displayed the column on the left side of the local news front page, where it still appears. The response from readers was so warm that, after six months, Gary began writing the column five days a week.

Thus began the career that led to this book, KAYS GARY, COLUMNIST, a career interrupted just once, in 1968, when Gary tried public relations for a North Carolina mountain development company, found he didn't like it, and returned to the newspaper and his readers.

For years, editors at The Observer talked about publishing some of Gary's columns in book form, but the initiative finally came last year from Sally Hill McMillan, president of Charlotte's East Woods Press. When she and I first talked, both of us were thinking of a "Best of Kays Gary" approach. Some of Gary's colleagues—Perspective editor Ed Williams, columnist Dot Jackson, and associate

editor Jack Claiborne—helped sort piles of yellowed clip-
pings and reviewed microfilm for missing columns.
Readers sent in favorites they had saved. It soon became
obvious that there was no way to pick out the "best" work
of such a gifted and versatile writer. We settled for this collection that we think represents both variety and ex-
cellence.

It is not easy to write about Kays Gary. He is a complex
man. Reared in the small town of Fallston, 10 miles north
of Shelby on Highway 18 to Morganton, he grew up in the
Great Depression. His father, W. R. Gary, was a small, wiry
man with a shock of thick, black hair that turned white
early, perhaps from the strain of instilling quality and
high morale into the low-budget school of which he was
principal. His mother was a teacher and taught Gary to
read when he was four. It was in those early years that
Gary developed his respect and love for the English
language, his precise knowledge of grammar and the fine
shading of meanings between words often used by others
as synonyms.

He read all the books he could find. Though short and
stocky, he played basketball and baseball. He got to know
the kids and their parents in the nearby communities of
Cherryville and Belwood and Casar and Polkville and to
this day understands better than anyone else at The
Observer the readers who live and work in the smaller communities of the Piedmont.

It was there, also, that he came to know the hardships
of the Depression—grinding poverty among the red clay
cotton farmers and underpaid textile workers of northern
Cleveland County. He saw there also how neighbors shared
what they had with others less fortunate, a memory that
has inspired many of his efforts to help people and promote
good causes.

He went to college at Mars Hill and then on to Chapel
Hill and a 1942 degree in journalism, service in the U.S.
Army's Military Police until 1945 and his first full-time
newspaper job on the Shelby Daily Star. And what a job! He
was sports editor and columnist, county courthouse
reporter, feature writer, correspondent for The Charlotte
Observer (they were called "stringers" back then), local
news announcer for the Star-owned radio station WOHS,
play-by-play network announcer for the Western Carolina
Baseball League which he had helped organize, founder of
recreational youth programs for Shelby youngsters. He

worked seven days and nights a week and loved it.

By the time he was offered a job at The Observer in 1952, three of his Star colleagues had already moved on—Dick Young Jr. to The Charlotte News, Jay Jenkins and Bob Brooks to the Raleigh News & Observer, all three becoming outstanding journalists. In those days, The Shelby Daily Star was to turn out many successful graduates. The Star's philosophy of hard work, lots of it, and speedy writing under great pressure produced good craftsmen, even if the pay was low.

Gary recalls well his first week in the more leisurely Observer newsroom. Fretful and frustrated after several days with no assignment, he was finally told to interview a resident of Dilworth who had just returned from Alaska. "I wrote 40 inches about that man when 10 would have done it," he recalls. Gary's early columns often used "People and Politics" as the lead item, followed by several shorter sections of odds and ends, labeled "City Side," "Public Business," "Cuff Stuff," plugs for events that would not make the paper otherwise, and "The Littl'uns," cute sayings of kids sent in by teachers, mothers and grandmothers.

Somewhere along the way, and no one is quite sure when or why, Gary began to develop the longer essay—an entire column devoted to a single person or event or cause or idea. Although he is usually calm, soft-spoken and reflective, Kays has a boiling point. When he writes in a rage, his anger is terrible, his words can be brutal. Fortunately most of those out-of-character columns were held back by editors, either because Kays was too overwrought or the subject matter belonged on the editorial page.

Most of the time he is just plain Kays Gary—a modest, humble and unselfish man who cares deeply for people, especially those who need a helping hand. Gary writes so feelingly about unhappiness and tragedy because he has known both in his personal life. He writes with equal passion about joy and ecstasy for he has known them, too. And when he describes a peaceful mountain cove, his prose becomes poetry. Unlike many journalists who tend to become jaded and cynical, Gary is still starry-eyed about human nature, our society and the newspaper business.

Gary's work habits are illogical. At one point, we gave him a private office so he could avoid the noise and distractions of the newsroom. It didn't work. He moved back to a desk in the middle of the newsroom, cluttered with notes

and scraps of paper, with telephones ringing and type-
writers clacking all around him, cigarette ashes all over
the place. He was at peace again. He could concentrate.

Tom Fesperman, long-time managing editor of The
Observer, recalls another of Gary's work habits:

"One thing I remember about Gary was that he was
late. He was dependable that way: Gary's column was going to be late. I used to push the deadlines up on him, make
him think that he was not going to get into the paper if he
didn't get the column in earlier. It never fazed him. He
turned it in at the same old time, late.

"He didn't do it just to drive editors mad; he never put
that much of a value on editors. He did it because he was
busy trying to absorb the whole community around him.
He mulled over the mail. He called people on the phone. He
greeted visitors like a receptionist and questioned them
like a head-shrinker. He considered items and rejected the
flat ones. Then when he was overloaded with lore, or
somebody's hand-wringings, or his own emotional reac-
tions to the high and mighty, or more frequently the low
and the weak, and when the sun was close to the ground,
then he was ready to let some of it out. And here it came, a
sort of tropical shower of words, late but warm."

Finally, a Gary quality that ranks along with his
writing skill and his compassion is his reporter's eye for
detail. In the words of Ed Williams:

"When you come to the point where you need a keen
eye for observation, Gary always has it. It's all there. And,
when he's telling a story at its best, it's as though the
writer is not even between you and what's going on. He is
so skillful and so clean and sharp and direct, you don't get
the feeling that you are reading writing; you feel that
you're having an experience. That's the kind of writing
that makes you cry."

In 1969, when Gary left The Observer for his fling at
public relations, I wrote:

"It should also be noted that in losing Kays Gary, the
humanitarian, the newspaper business is also losing a
great reporter—and there are not many of them around.

"Reporting is the most basic of journalistic skills, yet
relatively few men who work at this trade would be called
great by their colleagues.

"Gary is one of them. The sharp eye for fine detail, a
full range of strong action verbs, the ability to describe persons and places, the capacity for capturing a mood, the

facility for organizing facts quickly and in good order, sometimes under great deadline pressure—these are but a few of the qualities that make a good reporter.

"Gary has them and more. And I in no way mean to diminish his humanitarianism and its importance when I salute him as a truly great reporter."

You will not find in this collection some of the great stories that Kays Gary wrote—stories that readers still talk about . . . "Long Sam," Mae McRacken, Virgilio Pinto, Victor (The Little Pony) Palomino, Annette Robinson, "Eddie is Dead." These are most prominent in the memories of long-time Gary readers, and intense interest in each was sustained through many columns.

These stories are not here because they continued for weeks and months and no single column dealt adequately with them.

What you will find are over 60 Kays Gary columns, selected by his colleagues as representative of his good works. We hope you will enjoy rereading and reliving them.

Big newspapers tend to become institutions—impersonal, caught up in the affairs of politicians and celebrities, preoccupied with national and international crises, sometimes forgetful that among their readers are thousands of good, loyal, hard-working people who find it increasingly difficult to cope with the simple business of living and surviving. Through the years Kays Gary has stayed in touch with those people. He has listened to them, he has helped them, he has made them laugh, he has made them cry.

A friend once remarked that The Charlotte Observer made Kays Gary what he is. In truth, Kays Gary has helped make The Charlotte Observer what it is.

C. A. (Pete) McKnight, 1981
Editor, The Observer
(1955-76)

Bleeding Heart Stories

A long time ago, when we were in the old building, Kays used to have a desk in what we called "The Bay of Pigs." It was a space with about five desks, set off by a bannister. Harriet Doar and Gene Payne sat in there, along with Dick Banks and a couple of others.

Every morning the line would form along the bannister, waiting to see "Mr. Gary." Mr. Gary could cure the sick and feed the hungry and right all wrongs. All the time Mr. Gary would also be counseling the afflicted on the telephone and pleading the orphan's case by mail and digging into his own pocket. Somehow, every day he also wrote a column.

Well, he left us in the summer of '68. He wrote his goodbye column, and then he came back in, sometime around midnight. He had been packing up to move to Beech Mountain. I remember he had on some old dungarees, and a grimy tee shirt with a hole in it, and some ratty tennis shoes, and a stiff drink under his belt.

"I want to talk with you," he said. "I'm afraid they're going to offer you my job. Don't take it. Tell 'em the hell with it. If you get into what I got into you'll never be a writer as long as you live. You'll get so mixed up in people's troubles you'll go crazy. . . ."

So what did he do? He got out of it and he nearly went crazy. In two years, he was back, carrying the weight of the world. Kays never wanted to be a "bleeding heart." The thing was, when somebody came to him for help, he never could say no. He helped, because he couldn't help it. . . .

I like what Ed Williams once said, that Kays is that "Somebody" we mean when we say, "I wish Somebody would help those kids," or "Somebody ought to do something for those old people." Kays, Ed said, ought to have a big S on his chest—for "Somebody."

Dot Jackson

Blood Relations

He was scrawny for a 10-year-old but he sat on the front row bench of Domestic Relations Court and tried to look like a man.

There were six other people in the room besides the judge who sat behind a desk 'way up high.

There was a lady in a blue suit who sat beside the boy and patted him on the shoulder.

Behind a table to his right sat a man and woman with whom he'd lived a long, long time.

Yes, he had said, he loved them. He sure did. He was all they had. They didn't have any kids of their own.

And facing him, in a chair on a platform, was a third woman in the room.

She was the modern Magdalene. She'd had two husbands at the same time and many boy friends. She also had three children and the eldest and scrawniest of these she had tossed to the man and woman who now sat behind the table.

Now the husbands were gone and the boy friends were gone. The days were long and the nights longer and, she vowed with shuddering sobs, now she was changed. She wanted her son.

Ten-year-old eyes never left her as she poured out her soul on the witness stand.

The return of custody on a temporary, trial basis, said the judge, was largely dependent on the wishes of the child.

They waited the verdict. The boy looked long at the man and woman behind the table.

Then he walked toward The Magdalene. She threw herself into his bony arms. Her eyes were fountains of tears. His were deep wells of mercy.

Even as they left, his arm around her, he walked very straight . . . for this is the way a man of responsibility must walk . . . when he becomes the head of a family.

1958

One Precious Possession

Disaster comes in several sizes and not always is it measurable.

This is a truth delivered with the impact of a cannon shot upon visiting Mrs. Harriet Hudson, 79.

She sits in a three-room shanty just south of Matthews. Also in the shanty are her daughter, son-in-law and six grandchildren.

She has been there a week, now, for it has been a week since The Wind.

Until The Wind, she had owned—besides her memories—six precious things.

Five of them are gone.

There had been an organ, an old imitation fur coat, a family Bible, a cook stove and a picture.

They were in another three-room shack, 500 yards down the road, when The Wind came.

It was the place where she had lived, piecing together bits of cloth now and then for quilts.

But on the afternoon of The Wind, she had been here.

After it was over and the blackness had gone from the skies, Harriet Hudson found only a front wall and a front door standing.

Gone was The Coat.

"Mama set up that coat as the grandes' thing that ever was," said daughter Lola. "She never wore it none much. She mos'ly looked at it. Papa give it to her a long, long time ago at Christmas.

"It was bad times and they was 11 children and I 'member she said, 'Papa you done paid too much for me a coat'."

Gone was the stove. Crushed beneath a chimney.

"Mama had to always be cookin' up fo' us an anybody that come by. When she got that 'namel wood range you'd a thought she'd got the world!"

Gone was the picture.

"It was the only one of Papa, the reverend of the Methodist Church. Papa, he was knowed by ever'body and growed up with the Caldwells and was with 'em 65 years to when he died three year ago.

"Papa, mama always said, "knew The Word back'ards and for'ards.""

Gone was the organ and the Bible.

"She play the organ for hymns and praises to the Lord. It was 30 years old and more. The organ it was a crownin' glory in the house of a preacher and the children didn't mess with bangin' on it.

"The Bible has all us names and birthdays and Mama, she proved everything by it. No tellin' where it got blown to."

Harriet Hudson, chin resting on hands clasped atop a cane, murmured now and then, staring at the wall.

"The Lord giveth," she said once, "an' the Lord taketh away."

"Mama," put in daughter, Lola, "had a light stroke a good many years back, and she can't seem to understand things and get 'em straight!"

The Red Cross had come. A committee in the community would be asked to recommend what sort of help Harriet Hudson should get.

The Red Cross might come again but it would not bring The Picture, The Coat and The Organ.

And so a question was asked her:

"Why do you think the Lord would take from you?"

And she said: "I don't s'posed to know. I trusts Him."

And here was the sixth precious thing Harriet Hudson had owned and had not lost—her faith.

July, 1956

Detective Jack

Sometimes you wonder whether Detective Jack should not get out of the policing business and into social work.

At other times, such as when some tough thug decides to resist arrest, you are not sure about this. At such times Detective Jack does not remind you of your gentle old grandmother.

But for every "client" he would like to see en route to Alcatraz with a one-way ticket, there is another for whom he turns himself inside out. Himself and his pockets.

Detective Jack is turned inside out again. This time it is over a lady who turned up on a bad-check rap.

She bought groceries with the bad check. Because of this, Detective Jack wants a look-see at the rest of the setup.

And the setup is two small people, ages 5 and 2, and a husband and herself and $70 a month.

But the kicker is that the lady has cancer, but not nearly as bad as her husband, who is not long from reaching the point that groceries will be the least of his worries.

Naturally, Detective Jack and the other tough cops drop by now and then with grub and things of one kind or another but the trick is to make the $70 go further.

The family occupies a furnished apartment—lousy furnishings, to be sure, but furnished, and this takes more than half the $70.

He has lined up another apartment and a better one at that for $22.50 and has latched onto a stove here and a refrigerator there but things are moving sorta slow.

He hated to ask but did we reckon we could ask folks to find some bedding and chairs and stuff like that?

We reckoned. So call us.

It is time Detective Jack got back to catching robbers and writers of bouncing checks and bad people like that.

September 6, 1959

'Cabby Mack'

It happened at the intersection of Providence and Queens roads and when it was over Cabby Mack was ready to turn in his chauffeur's license. His real name, I shall tell you, is not Mack.

"I could-a crawled in the ground and covered myself up," he said, "but then I give it another good think.

"I decided if maybe I push this cab another million miles around Charlotte, maybe I will learn something about people."

This was some confession because Cabby Mack, a solid citizen himself, can haul a fare six blocks and tell you what he is made of.

There are police who can testify to his uncanny ability to spot phonies, cheapies, chippies and blue-chip citizens in no time at all.

Up to this Christmas season moment.

It had begun four nights earlier. The fare was a man, a desperate-looking man. He wanted to go to the intersection of Queens and Providence.

There he just commanded Cabby Mack to stop. They sat there. Just sat.

Finally, after a long time, the man said, "Let's go."

The next night it was the same. And the next. There was something more than desperation about the man—something almost pathetic—and yet he did not want to talk.

"Cabby Mack" sat there looking at the supermarket and drug across the way—the crowds of Christmas shoppers. He thought of the heavy cash there.

"I got to buy a pack of cigs," he said. "Be right back."

The man did not seem to hear.

Mack called police. They got there in a hurry. They wanted to know the story. They got it.

The man pointed to the window of Myers Park Methodist—the mighty and beautiful back-lighted stained glass window.

"That's it," he said. And he looked down at his hands, his tightly clasped hands, and told the rest.

"I have never been much on religion. I didn't know how to pray. My wife . . . they tell me at the hospital things are going mighty rough.

"And then I found the window. Something about it gives me the strength and the peace—the feeling and the words to pray . . ."

That is all to the story except . . .

If you are lucky on some evening at dusk you may see a cab pause at the curb of Providence and Queens.

The driver will be alone—a driver who had passed the place 10,000 times without seeing The Window until the moment of his massive mistake.

It was not only the biggest—it was the best mistake Cabbie Mack ever made.

December 18, 1958

Bicycle Lessons

The letters came on the eve of Christmas eve.

The boy, 12, wrote his with a pencil. His sister, 10, wrote hers with a pen. They gave their addresses and phone numbers, and both were addressed, precisely, to me.

Each letter said the mother had only enough money to pay rent and buy food. Each asked that I intervene with Santa Claus to bring them 10-speed bikes and an electric game.

The letters boggled me, infuriated me, saddened me. But I had to reply:

Dear Tommy and Amanda: I received your letters, and I will have a word with Santa Claus, but I must tell you something else—Santa doesn't always do what I ask. And you know what? I believe in him, anyway. He has a way of making up at some time for all the wishes gone astray.

You want a 10-speed bike? I don't blame either of you. I remember. Boy, do I ever.

Every year for a long time I carried in the pocket of my bib overalls a picture of a red bike with balloon tires. Tore it out of Sears. They didn't have 10 speeds back then, but they did have coaster brakes, which was a pretty hot item.

I never got that bike. I knew I wouldn't get it. My father asked me if I didn't know that he'd buy it for me if he could afford it. I said, "Yes" and meant it. And I told him a fib. I said I really didn't want a bike. I wanted a basketball.

Each year my father would take me with him on mud roads around Sugar Hill and off N.C. 18 around Buffalo Creek. He had the back of the car full of bags of oranges, some coffee and boxes of stick candy.

He knew all the people in the houses. Their kids went to the school where he was principal. They went, that is, when they weren't sick.

Those houses were mighty cold. You could see the ground through the floor. Sometimes there were chickens running around in the houses. Even today I remember the babies crying, wheezing with every breath, their noses running. Their diapers were wet. The smells were bad.

In those houses my father would talk to everybody in there a little while about school and stuff, and then he'd say to the mother or father: "Well, I brought the stuff you ordered from the store. It's out in the car.''

And outside he'd tell the father some folks in town had given him the stuff.

"It's your mother's idea," he'd tell me. "She could have had a new coat." And one year he said, "Well, there went your bike."

Your mother can't buy 10 speeds for you because she can barely buy food and pay the rent?

I know a little bit about that. I remember the night I saw my father crying. He didn't know I saw.

I was maybe 11 years old, and I woke up in the night and saw a light under the kitchen door, and I tiptoed to it in the dark and looked through the key-hole where the sound was coming from.

My father was sitting at the kitchen table where he did his figuring and my mother was standing in her bathrobe behind him with her hands on his shoulders and he was talking about owing the bank and Stamey Company and being out of coal.

If I had the world's finest bicycle at that moment I would have sold it to make him stop crying.

So I never got the bicycle. I got a lot of things better.

I can still wish. If I had it, the wish, the hope, would be gone. And I would be very old.

That is why my main fun comes every year around Dec. 11 with the Great Bike Giveaway when almost 100 kids get their first bikes. They're used, mostly, but I know a secret. No matter what the future holds, new bikes, cars or whatever, none will ever match the thrill of the first bike.

Next year, if Santa doesn't come through this time, I'll see you there.

Meanwhile, let me clue you in on a deal for the happiest Christmas.

Your mother is probably down because she can't help Santa get those bikes. If she did you wouldn't have enough to eat, and your house wouldn't be warm. She hurts from needing to give more than she has when she is giving it all.

This is your chance to learn a secret of happiness most of us wish we'd learned much earlier and some of us never learned. It's the secret of giving.

Enclosed is a $10 bill. It won't buy a bike or even a bicycle wheel, but you can use it to give to your mother or anybody else who has given you love.

Watch her face. You will never forget. It will be, I promise, the Christmas you will remember better than all the Christmases that have been and all the Christmases to come.

Merry Christmas, Tommy and Amanda, and a Happy New Year full of 10-speed wishes!

December 24, 1976

Real Estate Man

It was Mack's voice on the 'phone from his real estate office.

"I need help," he said. "I do not want to sell this house."

"For a real estate man," I tell him, "it sounds like you've come a crop of rocks in the cranium."

"Don't joust me, word man," retorts Mack. "Let me make my spiel!"

So he made it.

It had been a slow week. But the sun comes out on a Thursday and his 'phone rings and the man says: "I want you to sell my house for me."

So he loses no time kicking his four-year-old Ford out there.

At first he feels let down because it is not a layout of the type which would carry a name . . . like "Pine Haven."

It shrieks $8,000 but it is neat and should turn over very fast and so he feels better until the guy answers the door.

He is in a wheelchair.

There are greetings back and forth and Mack allows that before they talk business they had better summon the little woman, ha-ha, because you know you can't make and deal without 'em!

But the guy in the wheelchair—and he is a very big guy about 44—looks at one big hand very carefully and says the little woman is not there and has not been there for six months and will not be back. In fact, he says, there is no one to talk business but him.

Moreover, says the guy, the business at hand is not the mightiest transaction since his equity in the house . . . well, he has been making payments on it.

Mack does not see that the big guy is playing the right percentages because he has got to live some place and his equity is not going to carry him a far piece.

He insists on the how comes.

All right, says the guy, but he does not see how this will affect the price of houses.

Multiple sclerosis happened. Six, seven years ago. It crept up and knocked him into a wheelchair and out of the grocery business but there are many ways for a slowly dying man to make a living.

So he buys a truck and hires a driver who will lift him into the truck and they go around buying old batteries and selling them for rebuilding.

Four years this goes on so that he makes a living and makes the house payments and buys another truck. This is the American Way. Grow. Expand.

Last fall the battery business begins to go bust. He sold one of his trucks. Last winter batteries, businesswise, just died and stayed that way.

That's when the little woman left. In the night. A sun came up and she was gone.

Last spring he and the driver hauled produce around and about almost making ends meet. But now there is no produce to haul or, it seems, anything else and the house payments are getting rougher.

"And that's it?" said Mack.

"That's it," says the guy, looking out the window.

"What about that '56 truck out there?" Mack wants to know.

"It needs something to haul," the big man said, "but I can't find it. I guess it will pay my keep in a nursing home for awhile."

This was Mack's spiel. He said he was through. That is the reason he does not want to sell the guy's house. There must, he said, be a way.

"It's rough," I tell him. "It's life."

"The hell it is," says Mack.

We'll see.

1957

Little Mr. Kim

Goodbye, Mr. Kim, and thanks for the Christmas message. Seriously, we needed that. And if we have not achieved peace on earth, brotherhood and all that, you helped us work on it.

Three weeks ago, sir, we didn't know you. Not many of us, anyway, and the few who did were only individually impressed with the curious, courteous, humble oriental manner of a little immigrant. You were, sir, a momentarily arresting subject of interest—you with your Bible and hymnal under arm, bowing and "Very very thank you-ing" everybody you met, even the busy officer who issued your driver's license.

And then, just a few hundred yards from your rented room near Raleigh, you had to get yourself killed by a car in the night and take up all this space in the paper because of problems of what to do with the body of a broke mechanic from the other side of the world. Here are remains with an estimated worth of 98 cents, before inflation, placed into cold storage because of a $2,000-plus price tag on sending such a small package home.

This, to say nothing of potential funeral costs when all you left was an envelope in your coat pocket containing $45 and marked "Contribution For God's Work."

Some legacy, that.

Naturally questions had to have answers and slowly they evolved—how you and your Christian convert family back in Inchon, Korea, had gone off the deep end about the Savior with some other equally impoverished neighbors and a wild idea about buying land and building a church. It all came out about the praying bit on coming to America and getting a job to make more money to get the church job done first.

Oh, yes, we even learned that Neuse Baptist, the first church you could get to, found you there every time the doors opened giving prayers of thanks about the coming-to-America prayers being answered. But it was almost too much to learn that your first $100 earned here had been sent to that church instead of your wife and three kids. In this day and time one learns to look after No. 1 first. It gave some relief to learn that you had instructed new friends to send 10 per cent of future grosses to the church, 60 per cent to the family and retain a whopping $30 a week for yourself.

Truthfully, sir, you've been a lot of trouble. You've bothered us something fierce lying here in cold storage and reminding us almost every day of an old story about self-giving and the meek inheriting the earth. All that.

You've left us, in the modern vernacular, "just hanging twisting slowly, slowly in the wind."

You made widows on Social Security send in dollars and people decide to send memorials to you instead of exchanging Christmas gifts. You've made brusque, "business-first" executives rip out check books in privacy and write out $100 checks, even forgetting to write in "Contribution" for tax purposes.

You caused those fellow-worshipers at Neuse Baptist, from redneck to scholar, to decide to build that little church in Korea in the next year when they're already supporting missionaries.

Saturday, a funeral director took your body out of cold storage and gave it the VIP treatment and how do you like the new blue suit? Beautiful casket. No charge.

And then other funeral directors of Raleigh, Wake Forest, Zebulon and Apex sent word that they'd buy your ridiculously priced airline ticket home.

Over at Neuse Baptist the mail was still coming in and Rev. Hugh Carey and Rev. M. L. Walters were still counting money, just over $4,000. And in Seoul, Korea missionaries have advised that $5,000 invested for your family will yield a thumping 24 per cent interest. The interest alone will give them a better living than they've ever known.

Ah, Mr. Kim, that smile on your face is not as inscrutable as it is supposed to be.

Undoubtedly, little man, you know that you've shown us something that you knew all along.

So you are leaving Monday.

You will be home in plenty of time to celebrate the Birthday of the Child who claimed such single minded devotion.

That Star in the East will shine a little brighter this year. And maybe we'll really hear those herald angels singing.

Goodbye Mr. Kim.

December 9, 1973

Promotion Wanted

He wasn't promoted to second grade.

Can you imagine what that's like to a six-year-old?

It's like getting fired from your first job.

It's more than that, I'll tell you.

On the average of one night every two weeks for 15 years I've had a nightmare. The same one over and over. It started when I was faced with the prospect of writing a play in one night or failing to graduate from college.

I wrote it and I made it. But since then I dream that I have been in college for 15 years lacking only the play to graduate and the diplomas are always handed out before I can finish the play.

It's torment. I dread that dream like death.

Not being promoted to second grade, then, is worse than that.

It happened to little Gary Nash of Whitney, near Spartanburg, S.C. And that isn't all.

He has been a semi-invalid since he was 2 and fell on his head from a moving car. Gradually, he is losing control of his motor muscles. This, plus measles and chicken pox, made him miss a lot of school that first year.

He came home from school with children trailing him calling him a "baby" for his failure. He opened his book and read for his mother and counted to her to prove to her and himself he was smart enough for second grade.

But finally he said he would not go to school again.

Since then he has been sicker and sicker and he has received three get-well cards and he reads them over and over and asks his mother why he doesn't have more cards and there was a story in the Spartanburg Herald, so maybe he has some now.

Just now Gary has been taken to the Medical College of Charleston, if you'd like to send cards there. Maybe the doctors and cards will help.

But there is something else I wish they would do, though logic might dictate it unwise:

I wish they'd promote Gary Nash to the second grade. Now.

September 10, 1957

The Little Walking Man

Things have changed for The Little Walking Man.

No longer is he wretched, a creature of misery plodding dumbly along survival's ragged edge. The Little Walking Man is a person now and he knows it, if humbly.

And this was the highlight of a mountain weekend, seeing him like this. It left something to wonder about warmly, something to sing inside about, something to stir the innermost in a manner almost forgotten.

The Little Walking Man. Travelers of the Boone area and of highways in Watauga and Avery counties know him. Name is "Buck." For years his twisted, bent figure, pushing his wheelbarrow, has been as familiar as the roadside billboards and the mountains themselves. He picks up bottles, tossed by motorists into the ditches. Area merchants give him pennies for the bottles. With the pennies he buys things to eat, thus gaining the energy to pick up more bottles.

For years the face of The Little Walking Man has been mostly the face of pain and his manner that of a whipped stray—hungrily, cringingly scavenging the roadsides.

"Buck" cannot speak. He emits grunting sounds which seem mostly to be questions never really answered. His facial muscles have long seemed contorted in a spasm of, if not despair, a hunger never satisfied. In winter months the cold compounds this, the bitter winds freezing, then chapping and leaving raw his mouth and chin from the trickling saliva.

"Buck's" head has always been bowed most of the time. When he lifted it, no one could escape the pleading look of his close-set eyes and yet how could one respond to it?

Some responded with coins and some with favors such as would be tossed to any miserable creature of the roadside.

And some would respond with cruelty. There are the stories of younger men who had great fun by catching him, stripping him naked in the bitter cold and riding away to toss his overalls over an embankment. There are too many stories like that.

But I remember a snowy November night more than 10 years ago when Buck proved to me he was a man and more.

A knock sounded at the door of Floyd Ayers near Valle Crucis and we wondered what manner of man would be out in such a night. It was "Buck," agitated, twisting and turning and making those grunting sounds. He plucked at Floyd's clothing, obviously beckoning us to come.

It was a fearsome, freezing trip, down the mountain, across a stretch of pasture bottomland and a clawing, sliding climb up another mountain with "Buck's" gruntings getting more urgent.

And then we found it—a calf—its head and neck caught, twisted in barbed wire fencing, so weak it could no longer bawl out a cry of distress. We managed to free it. "Buck" nodded his head, clapped his hands and the look on his face was the nearest I'd ever seen to a smile. And off he went into the blizzardy night.

That was a time when "Buck" showed he was more than a dumb creature. There was the revelation that his being held a strength and a virtue beyond that of most of us. The mind literally reeled with the impact of what "Buck" had done, feeding fires of wonder at what really lay locked inside The Little Walking Man.

But memories fade. "Buck" has simply remained a part of the landscape, uncomfortable to be around up close. He had, of course, no training in self-care and hygiene.

On the mountain weekend I'd given no thought to "Buck" as Betty Jean and I visited with John and Mrs. Perry, owners of a cluster of new shops, including the Red Roof Restaurant alongside Highway 105 six miles out of Boone. The former vice president of Cannon Mills and his bride have just opened their place on the banks of the rushing Watauga and we had just finished lunch when a vaguely familiar figure entered.

He was noticed because other diners were in Sunday trappings or the expensive casuals of travelers while he wore spanking new overalls. He was freshly barbered, clean-shaven and some must have wondered if, in such surroundings, he would not experience some embarrassment. But two smiling waitresses immediately greeted him and led him to a table.

There was something about his walk, the jerking movements. . . .

"Is that . . .?"

I never finished the question. John Perry said, "That's Buck, all right."

Con Yates, an electrical contractor up the road, had

been mostly responsible for the change. The Perrys had helped.

"Some people have remarked that it didn't look too good with him in here but I've told them I'm sorry. Buck gets to eat at his own table."

Buck sat, picked up his napkin, kept touching it to his mouth to keep it free from spittle. He sat very still and as straight as he could and when they brought his food, he smiled a big smile and nodded happily to everybody.

"Con fixed a shower for him at his place and when he gets all cleaned up he knows he can come over and eat if he's hungry," Perry said. "Seems to us that Buck is smarter than his old appearances."

With every bite Buck seemed to give everyone in the room a look of friendly thanks. It was the highlight of a mountain weekend.

                                        August 14, 1973

Gratitude

Feeling depressed? A little sorry for yourself?

Two small stories may alter the perspective.

The first came from a doctor, a Friday night dinner companion toying with his food.

It had been a long, tiring day with no disappointments. His most seriously ill patient survived surgery and yet the doctor was not swept with relief. It was another feeling, an awesome and humbling feeling, a feeling beyond these words that was not dismissable.

"The quality of gratitude," he said, "or the quality of compassion some people own is, uh, something not easy to understand. You would think there is a limit."

And bit by bit he spoke of his patient, an old man without family who lost everything except 30 heartbeats a minute. Or so it seemed.

He lost a leg. Arteriosclerosis took his memory, his reasoning. He had long been blind. Congestive heart failure left him gasping with those 30 heartbeats a minute. Only a pacemaker could give him a measure of relief and life.

There was something about the old man, a gentle dignity, an indefinable quality of graciousness, whispered monoysyllabic words of acceptance and trust and agreement that commanded life. Words like "Yes," "Thank you," with a small and quivering smile.

The doctor was not sure the old man could understand anything about what was to be done, the risks. Reasoning blocked, eyes blinded, there were only repeated words, attempts at simple explanation of a complex condition. The old man could only smile and nod.

And so the surgery was done, the pacemaker implanted. The heartbeat was steady. In the recovery room, finally, the old man was conscious as the doctor stopped in.

His first words were: "I can see!".

"He knew we were trying to help him," the doctor said. "That is all he understood. He didn't want to disappoint us. He can't see."

The doctor was quiet again and I didn't bother to press the matter even as a silent question began to grow:

Does the old man see in a way the rest of us cannot?

Story No. 2:

Lettie M. Gary is 81, her life spun out in loving and teaching children and her own small family. Like the old man, never a complaint had she and never once a martyr. Her dinner plate commanded only chicken wings. Best pieces were for others.

I went to college on Mama's chicken wings and her make-do in restyling old clothes and reupholstering old furniture. Yet, in beauty and graciousness, she could impress any company.

And so it remained even when, some years ago, the hardened arteries took all but those qualities and commandments of simple presence.

Sometimes, when the faded blue eyes glimmer with smiling recognition, I wonder how much is still there, because she no longer has words enough. Nor have I.

Then came a fright on Friday afternoon. She'd had a fall and suffered a deep, ugly and profusely bleeding cut over her right eye. Yet, through all the experience of being lifted in and out of cars and being carried to the hospital for injections and stitches, her demeanor was as serene as if guests had dropped in for tea.

Was it possible that Mama, finally, no longer thought or felt anything?

The silent question was answered as I pushed her wheelchair through the hospital's parting electric doors.

The wheelchair went through smoothly but I stumbled and bumped my knee.

Mama said "Ouch!"

June 5, 1977

Big Roads Are Made
For Rollin'

You can really blow it out on the Big Roads. You sure
can let it roll on the big, wide, one-way concrete ribbons
with the median strips between. And on this night
everybody was rolling.

It was nice with the radio playing soft and the black
rubber smoothly spinning and you could scarcely hear the
powerful purr of the engine plunging you westward in the
early dark.

You had an almost sensual feeling of satisfaction with
the rightness of this big road and the easy, big, safe speed
while lounging in the bucket seat like a rocking chair at
home.

But just over the easy rolling rise and down the grade
ahead were flashing red lights. There were a lot of red
lights, flashing and spinning, and it would hit you that
somebody must have got caught really putting his foot
through the floor at about 90, maybe.

So you slowed and rolling down there you saw police
waving their flashlights and a crowd around and you
pulled to the side and got out.

There was this sheet spread on the grass of the median
strip and it was almost flat, just a little rumpled on the
grass, so you ask the nearest policeman there what
happened.

"Old man got hit. Old man got killed," he said, waving
that flashlight at the heads peering out of windows as cars
slowly rolled past.

Shelby Police Chief Knox Hardin came by with some officers carrying a metal tape measure and he was saying,
"Now measure from right here."

"Two hunnerd and eight fi' feet, that's how far he got
knocked," somebody said, and a policeman wrote it down
in a little book.

There were other voices in the night yellowed by the
lights of cars parked along the shoulders of the big road.

"This feller in the first car, he said he saw 'im comin'
onto the road and he slowed and swerved. . . ."

"Man in the station wagon couldn't-a seen him,
though. When the first feller slowed he just pulled out to

pass and 'WHAM'!

"Bet he didn' even know what he hit."

The officer with the flashlight glanced down at the sheet almost flat on the median grass. He reached down and lifted a corner.

"Know 'im?" he said.

The old, bronze face, old and dead, stared up and you looked away toward the side where a scuffed brogan and leg protruded crazily from the sheet. So little. So nothing. When the corner of the sheet flapped down it still looked flat.

"Wattie Jeeter. Some says he's 90 . . . some says 93 . . . some more'n a hundred. . . . Lived up there in that shack on an old truck bed. . . . Had him a wife who lives over yonder. . . . They say she quit living with him because he'd gone what she called 'quare'."

Down the Big Road several yards some people were standing around the front of a station wagon.

It bore the imprint of the tiny body, almost 18 inches deep into the grill and the hood and the windshield was shattered.

"It don't look possible such a little man could make such a big dent," someone said.

A little man and a big dent.

The men with the tape measure were still putting it down here and picking it up there.

Nobody asked who was Wattie Jeeter. What was to ask?

He lived up there in that shack he built on the bed of a truck and he had a bunch of dogs and his wife lived over yonder separate.

Wattie, he'd been around Shelby a long time.

One time, maybe 20 years ago, an officer remembered he'd been in court for something about selling some cotton seed. And others remembered seeing him scavenging for soft drink bottles he'd turn in at a fish camp for pocket money. Some even said they guessed at the fish camp that he'd come back and pick up the same bottles and sell them again the next day.

That's about all anybody knew except Wattie sure had been around Shelby a long time . . . 90, 95, 100 years.

The sheet still looked mighty flat on the grass.

About this time Wattie's wife, Mary, said to some folks at her house:

"Let's go pick up Wattie off the highway. He's done been run over."

Nobody had told her. They were just sitting there waiting for him to come to supper. He always came to supper she'd fixed even though they did live apart yonder. Nobody told her. It just came like a premonition.

"Let's go pick Wattie up off the highway," she'd said.

Hundred times, maybe, she'd told Wattie he was going to get run over crossing that road and Wattie always said, "I'm so old, ain't nobody goin' to run over me."

Mary and the folks would come over for picking him up and she would say, "Tain't so what they say about me and Wattie not getting 'long, mister. He was all I had. We been together right at 50 years."

The next day Mary would go up the bank and over yonder to the shack built on a truck bed to get out his "b'longings" but there wasn't much to take away. There was a skillet, though.

"Somebody stole his two best suits," she would say. "They come in here and stole his brown and blue suits."

She stood in the door holding that skillet and then looked up toward the heavens as if pondering the whereabouts of Wattie.

Oh, yes, she'd get a $40 grave and there'd be a funeral at the New Ellis Baptist Church.

Down there on the Big Road in the night with the red lights flashing and the officers measuring with their tape somebody had wondered if the biggest dent Wattie Jeeter had made on this world had been that ugly place in the front of the station wagon.

No, Mary said. No.

He'd sired five sons and four daughters and there were 30 grandchildren and 11 great-grandchildren and that was the truth.

Most of them would come to the funeral in the New Ellis Baptist Church, too.

But nobody had asked questions like that in the night with the red lights flashing. There wasn't time and there wasn't any need to ask questions like that. You have to get things measured and cleaned up and cleared out and it happened like that in about an hour.

Then the traffic could roll and it did roll.

The moon was just a little higher and it was a nice night with the radio playing softly and the black rubber spinning and the purring engine winging you westward while you lounged in the bucket seat just like the rocking chair at home.

You can really blow it out on the Big Road.

March 21, 1965

The Littl'uns

In Franklin last week a lightning bolt splattered trees in the C. W. Gidney yard, tossed debris on the roof, ripped a screen from a window and wrecked a sandbox.

Four-year-old Mark Gidney, momentarily stunned by the racket, recovered in time to conclude that "God pushed the button too hard."

Mrs. J. A. Postell likes to eavesdrop on the chatter of small fry who congregate on her paved driveway at 312 Lillington Ave. The latest: One little girl said she would be the policeman, a little boy said he would be the ambulance and another chose to be the fireman. "Now," said the little girl, "we need somebody to be dead."

September 10, 1957

Milestones Of Life

Kays Gary is a man of distilled wisdom who intrigues us with his insight and mellowed humaneness. He mesmerizes us with his prose and reveals to us the entanglements and complexities of this worldly earth and also overwhelms us with its beauty and goodness.

For many years I have eagerly read almost everything Kays has written, always to my profit. He sharpens our perceptions and heightens our enthusiasm by making us aware of life's flow. Kays has an eye for detail and the extraordinary descriptive powers of a writer that allows him to evoke vivid scenes and moods.

Kays Gary's writings make the commonplace become significant and the routine of life become memorable.

Jack B. Yarbrough, 1981
Aldersgate United Methodist Church
Shelby, North Carolina

Fathers

Fathers are . . .

Inadequate.

We never admit it except to ourselves but it is there. Fathers, no matter how fortunate or unfortunate the development of their progeny, have this feeling. Every father wishes he could start over because suddenly, one day, he is stunned to discover that there is no baby food in the grocery basket, no crackerjacks, no cereal with magic code rings inside.

Suddenly, the checks he signs are not for kindergarten but for college and wedding receptions and it is a shock. What happened?

It seems that he left them playing in the sandbox when he went down to the office on Saturday to catch up on some back work and when he came back . . .

Boom! The Band Aids and dirty sneakers and tricycles are gone and here are these young adults visiting.

It isn't fair. There was no warning. Was there?

But it is done and there is not much point in asking an aching question. But during his recent illness Harry Golden asked it of his eldest son.

"Have I been a good father?"

"Sure," Richard replied.

"You didn't waste any time thinking," said Harry. "Just because I'm in the hospital doesn't mean you have to be nice. What makes you so positive?"

Richard shrugged. "Hell," he said, "I'm forty years old. What difference does it make now?"

This exchange is a part of Harry's lead story, "How To Live With A Chair You Hate" in the June 17 edition of The Saturday Review.

This is the sad, sudden fact. All at once it is, "What difference does it make now?" Because every father knows, deep in his heart, that whatever he has been, it is not enough. Most especially, finding the sandbox set suddenly towering around and above him, he is acutely aware of the shabby exhibits of fatherhood about him—the color TV, the 397 cubic inch engine, the stereo, the credit cards.

And he wonders, with a tinge of bitterness, if "Captain Kangaroo" is a good father.

So this is what fathers think about or try not to think about on Father's Day when they put on the new tie and shirt. . . .

Or they should, if they are very young fathers. . . .

Because the day is inevitable when a father asks himself, "Have I been a good father?" And by the time he asks it he doesn't really want an answer. Instead, he looks around at the young adults no longer wearing jam on their faces and, most often, consoles himself with the thought that he is a lucky father . . . a most lucky father, indeed.

And besides . . .

Soon . . .

But not soon enough because the next years crawl . . .

There will be grandsons . . .

And baby food in the grocery basket once more. Plus crackerjacks. And cereal with a secret code ring inside.

Ah-hhhhh!

1964

A Lad's Small Voice

On an afternoon he is playing furiously.
Three hours later he is afire with fever.
Influenza, they say. Probably.
Two. Three. Four days.
He does not eat, now, nor drink.
He lies in semi-stupor, his flesh aflame.
To the hospital and fluids fed intravenously. Blood cultures. Five days. Six.
Virus undefined.
Seven days. Eight.

He lies there conscious but unanswering and an unending night is full of silent screams.

Nine days. The day brings dollar bills and bright cards, a football and games, fruit baskets, Mickey Mouse and Porky Pig on TV—all unreflected in the large, flat brown of his eyes.
Another long, long, untossed night is heavy with hunger for a sigh . . . a cry . . . a sign of restlessness.
The story of "Cootie," untold since he was only 3 and squirming in delight of it, is chanted in his ear and unheard.

And the soliloquy goes on . . . of Halloween and Christmas coming and a new bicycle . . . of the necessity, perhaps, of a doubled allowance.

Down the corridor footsteps quick, urgent and swiftly fading.
The length of him. Amazing. No child, really, at 11.
How did he get that way so soon? Sure, he played football and baseball and caught frogs and turtles and always, it seemed, chased about with a dog named "Choo-Choo."
But what else? What else, boy stranger?
The voice began again. It said there are even better things, maybe, than Christmas and bicycles. For instance, a man and a boy right away ought to get in the car and take two-three days down at the ocean. Fishing, mostly. Fishing in a boat and fishing off a pier.
Quiet.

Then a sound. Raspy and small but a sound . . . 11
years old.

"No girls?" It said. "Fishing with no girls?"
And the dawn, like the man said, came up like golden
thunder out of someplace.
. . . Some place where there's fishing. With no girls.

October 5, 1957

Off to College

She wasn't, thank heavens, my daughter.

Not that she didn't look nice. Heck, she looked like she had just waked up to find herself a princess.

But she was in the airport terminal alone. Going, no doubt, To College.

My daughter was at home paddling in mud puddles . . . or dumping a new box of cereal into a bowl to get the "s'prise" at the bottom . . . or catching frogs or helping tend to the puppies.

She'd just got back from seeing "Darby Gill And The Little People" and she had a box of popcorn and a Black Cow at the movie. And a boy with red pants pulled her hair.

But you wondered about this pretty little thing in the terminal.

Why was she alone? Changing planes, likely? Or had she sent her Mama and Daddy home because she wanted to leave All By Herself?

If she were MY daughter and she tried to send me home, I would spank her right there in the middle of the terminal, by gosh.

She was too young to be by herself.

The kids who go to college now!

She looked maybe 15 despite all the grown-up clothes and luggage. She had to be 18.

But look at her! New brown pumps—$20 if they cost a dime. And that cotton frock. Simple and designed to flatter the figure of a child who suddenly is a woman. It shrieked $45.

Beside her was a leather hat case. You know—like the models carry? You wondered if perhaps there might be a rag doll packed in there with the hat.

She was a portrait of studied sophistication.

Her legs are crossed just so, with the hem properly adjusted so that exactly enough of the billowy, lacy new petticoat is showing.

And they ought to be. She has been practicing enough here lately, you would bet.

She was thumbing through "Madamoiselle" magazine and not seeing a darned thing in it.

This is because people kept looking at her and smiling. It is hard to be sophisticated with people doing that.

She was worrying about that hem . . . or whether there was a green tag still hanging (HORRORS!) somewhere on the spanking new outfit.

Surreptitiously she glanced at the hem and touched the neckline while pretending to read the magazine—and she turned a brown pump just a little to make sure she hadn't stepped in anything.

Finally, she could stand it no longer. She picked up the hat case and walked (like Loretta Young, almost) toward a big glass door which had a reflection.

She stood there looking in the door. On the other side of the door was the rain. The sky was overcast and dreary out there.

Her back was to you when she fumbled around in her bag and brought out a handkerchief.

You hoped she was fixing her make-up.

With that damned lump coming up in your throat, you did your best not to guess that maybe she was dabbing at her eyes.

There was not a blamed thing to do except to get out of there . . .

And to phone your daughter to ask if maybe she'd caught any more frogs today.

September 3, 1959

But For A Merciful God And Good Brakes . . .

This will not be much of a column.

But then, except for a merciful God and good brakes there would be no column today, or ever again.

Instead there would have been a large Monday headline—because there were seven of us in the car.

By now the rains would have mingled the mud and the blood and the drainage ditches alongside Highway 53 six miles east of Winston-Salem would not show the difference.

Next month or next year a court would have awarded Mr. and Mrs. W. R. Gary, Fallston, N.C., age 63, thousands of dollars for the murder of their only child and their only grandchildren.

And the court would have to find somebody to award other thousands of dollars to for the death of David A. Holmes, his wife, Annie, their only child, a 16-year-old son.

This would have been difficult. David was brought up in an orphanage. Annie's mother and father are dead.

Beyond this circle it is not much of a family.

In the sum of man and his meanings this would not have made an eyewink of difference.

In the sum of those in this circle it would have meant the literal end of the world. We mean much to each other.

Bus drivers, I suppose, are the best drivers in the world. Their companies have the statistics to prove it.

But bus drivers, skilled as they are, are human. Humans make mistakes.

For one mistake made by one bus driver at 10:30 p.m. on a rainy Sunday night, I would, given the opportunity, have ripped his gullet from his throat with both hands.

My round Debbie was asleep probably. She always does. And often I look at her that way and wonder at her dreams.

The in-law Holmeses and their son were back there and Annie, terrified of the highway, anyway, had her glasses off so she would not see. Annie is chicken.

Because of her I was doing only 40 miles per hour. Because of her and because there was soft Brahms music on the radio.

Miss Boo was sitting next to me and the music had got the best of her and she was saying:

"I am glad I married you."

It was a strange time to say a thing like that for we have been married 15 years now. But then, I guess that is why we have been married 15 years.

My Billy was sitting in the front seat next to the door.

"You said I'd get indigestion, Daddy. I didn't get it. Uncle Julius tole me to order the shrimp cocktail. It cost more than my whole dinner yesterday, I betcha. He tole me to order the lobster, too. Uncle Julius is sure rich, isn't he, Daddy?"

That's when I saw the lights.

We were slowly climbing a hill. The lights were coming up the other side. I dimmed mine. We were just below the crest when something was suddenly wrong. A reflex told me there was a third light coming at us.

I jammed the brakes, cut to the shoulder.

In the same split second it was above us and on us—a monstrous, motorized, roaring mountain of a bus—passing a tractor-trailer on a curve at the crest of a hill.

Nobody screamed. It happened too fast to scream. A foot, two feet, perhaps even six feet it missed us and roared on into the rainy night on the downgrade at 60 to 70 miles per hour.

In seconds the windshield wipers had cleaned away the blinding cloak of muddy spray.

I barely remember stopping the car at a drive-in. I got out and walked around a while in the drizzle.

A while later we drove on. At 40 m.p.h. But on every curve and every hill there was that bus. It was there all night. It is there now. It will be there from now on and maybe this is good.

But somewhere I hope there is a driver of a nationally famous bus line who will read this and who will remember the car and will see it, too, on every hill and every curve.

Because there is not a bus, or bus line schedule in the entire world worth as much as a single breath of a daughter who still smiles in her sleep, of a son whose uncle might again one day buy him a lobster dinner . . . Or of a wife who will say again at some strange time and place:

"I'm glad I married you."

July 15, 1958

A Letter Is Priceless

There's something about a letter. . . .

We were all set to hoot, for lack of something else to hoot at in an indigestible hour, the folly of the latest Official Week—National Letter Writing Week.

To spend good money on hundreds of thousands of posters proclaiming it seemed such a waste . . . until . . .

I thought of letters saved in huge Manila envelopes . . . of letters in the desk . . . of letters in the attic. They're mine—the only treasures I ever saved. Mostly they're unanswered but not, surely, forever. They mean too much. Someday, when there are adequate words for gratitude . . . Someday . . .

He who writes a letter, a real one, gives of himself as he could in no other way. With pen in hand he is in a moment of truth he knows at no other time. He writes things he could never say. He dips his pen in his soul. He anoints you with it.

No Christmas gift was ever opened here more eagerly than a letter on a Monday—any Monday of any week in any year. It has ever been and will always be so.

Gifts can be bought, but not a letter. It is a priceless thing.

There is no reassurance like that of a letter.

Ask any man who ever waited in the rain for mail call on some foreign field. Ask any mother or mother's son or daughter whose heart beats only when the postman calls. Ask him whose letters are by the dozens daily. Ask him who gets none.

Watch glory transform a time-worn face as gnarled hands reach into some careful hiding place to draw out a well-worn letter.

Observe the child, age 4, when told: "You've got a letter."

The letter is among the things that matter most. It is a treasure and a debt and I am not bored now—I am bowed now—by Letter Writing Week. And someday, when there are words enough . . .

April, 1959

"Happy Mail"

With "Bus" Hatchell it's natchel; he just plain loves to deliver happy mail.

"Bus" is a Cheraw, S.C. postman who can identify happy mail just by the feel of it, the handwriting on the envelope and the name of the addressee. And the stuff gives him a glow. The happiest mail???

"Easy," says Bus. "Take Saturday morning, I ran into this old gentleman—about 90, he is—and he has been sick a lot for several years. But he was out strolling with his cane and I had a letter for him. It had a happy, hefty feel. I says to him, 'This looks like a good one,' and his face lights up like a Christmas tree.

"The letter is from a young couple, no kin, who left several years ago, but they always write him. 'I can't get over it,' said my friend. 'They're so young and I'm so old. You just don't see much of that these days—that kind of thinkin' of the old folks at home.' "

Well, sir, Bus said, that letter perked him up, too, and sent him home thinking up people he should write—people out of the past who need to know they're appreciated.

"I wish you'd get your readers to make this a special letter-writing week of that kind, Brother Gary," he said. "You'd have no trouble if you could see that old man's face. Besides, postmen dearly love to carry that happy mail!"

April 29, 1963

One Happy Letter

Observer General Manager J. E. Dowd just received a letter from his friend, "Bish" Colmore, who helps run the Philippine Mfg. Co. for Procter & Gamble in Manila. Colmore enclosed a letter he'd just received from a Chinese client. Here 'tis:

"Dear Friend:

"Your highness, may I request you to receive this my best reward, from my whole heartily delicated this humble personally letter for you, so Please. I wish, don't be worry, Sir, I am the oldest Chinese business man, my own responsible store in Cobu City, I am Yu Siu, I think.

"You're already know me, because your salesman always coming to my store, I was your friendship very long time.

"Well, your honor, I want to tell you my new address is Zamboanga City now 'cause I'm transfell here, for my newly era in place and I would like to traveling sales' at anywhere, so that this letter to let you know my another address to contenue to buy your stock as many.

"Now, best wishes and congratulation to your responsibelity and long live your productory!

"Very respectfully yours,

"YU SIU

"P.S. I thank you, Sir.

"I remain."

October 5, 1957

A Dog's Tale

"Black-Eye Susan" is her name, but it should be "Trouble" because that is what the frisky little Spitz has been for 17 years at the Henry Willard home on Briarcliff Road.

At an age when she should be dozing on the hearth, "Susan" still provokes turmoil and commands affection despite the tyranny she has imposed on the household.

Little Blanche Willard was five years old when Papa brought Susan home and created an alliance that was half unholy—Susan's half. Yet it prevailed through the years with Blanche as her adoring companion, protector and defense counsel.

Susan liked to nip ankles, almost any ankles except Blanche's. Susan built time in vet hospitals all over town—10 to 14 days at a crack—for simple assault.

On one occasion the dog catcher came by to commend the Willards for incarcerating Susan after a complaint. Maybe Susan detected a bit of insincerity in his voice. Anyway, she bit the dog catcher.

That was 10 years ago and Henry Willard decided that enough was enough. He took the seven-year-old Susan for what was intended to be a long, long sleep. En route Susan licked his face. Henry Willard drove and drove until, in Union County, he found a family willing to take her.

At home things did not go well. Mistress Blanche, then age 12, mourned and refused to speak. She began to carry her Bible with Susan's collar as a marker and filled the nights with prayers.

In one week, cockle-burred, scarred and sore, Susan limped across two counties and back to Briarcliff and little Mistress Blanche.

And for another decade the twosome prevailed.

Then came Halloween just over a month ago and the now-grown Blanche was in the midst of preparations for her wedding when Susan disappeared. The days and weeks went by and suddenly it seemed that tears would spring into Blanche's eyes at the mention of Susan's name.

Blanche and Michael Quinn were wed last Saturday and promptly started on their wedding trip to Gatlinburg, Tenn. En route, as newlyweds will, they lost their way some 85 miles from Charlotte on a back road. Dusk came swiftly and Blanche, peering for a road sign, gave a small cry and a one-word command: "Stop!"

Outside the car she called to the small figure trotting toward her but the little one was old and deaf. Not until they were only a few feet apart was there a hoarse bark. The small white dog with the black eye leaped into Blanche's arms.

And that is how Michael and Blanche Quinn came to spend their wedding night in the mountains with a little, old, indomitable, exasperating, lovable dog named Susan.

They brought her all the way back to Charlotte Sunday before continuing on their honeymoon.

Susan is quieter now on Blanche's old pillow.

In a day or two she'll be doing time at the vets again getting vitamin shots and all that in preparation for the Quinns' return and their move to Columbia, S.C.—the three of them.

Meanwhile, the Henry Willards eye the smug Susan and try to figure it out.

Maybe the old dog has just seen too many Walt Disney movies on TV . . . Or maybe that Bible with the dog collar book mark . . .

December 2, 1965

Easter

It is the time of the bud and the blossom and the bug and the bird.

It is the time of sunrise assault on winter's dumbness of man and land.

It is the time of the bursting bean and of murmured secrets in the earth.

It is the time of the turning worm, of new-wine breezes and white teeth tossing teased laughter at the sun.

It is the time when the silent egg proclaims its might with shattered shell—mightier than the Big-Big Bomb.

It is the time of the lifted fog and the unfettered promise . . . of the opened cell and the quick, sure stride.

It is the time of the surge and the thrust . . . of unceilinged flight and of songs and the rhyme.

It is the time of unforgetting . . . of sweetened breath . . . and forevered tomorrows.

It is the time of finished waiting . . . of eager, trembling certainty.

Soon, now.

It is the time of Yes.

It is Easter.

April 17, 1965

The "Last" Column

It is Saturday afternoon and while people are watching and winning and losing football games I am tranquilized to the teeth because the moment is here from which there is no escape.

It is the last column.

I have not allowed myself to think about it because there is too much to say and no time to say it even if I sat here and pounded the typewriter, uninterrupted, for another decade. After almost 23 years as a newspaper reporter, six with The Shelby Daily Star and 16 years, nine months and five days with The Charlotte Observer, I am moving into another world and how does one explain that?

The explanation, barren because it really is a small part, is that at age 47 the bells of opportunity are not scheduled to ring many more times.

A man has but one life to spend and it is not enough and there is the terrible urge to save it and to see if he can match some other challenge.

I am taking leave of The Charlotte Observer which is doing great things for the Carolina-Caribbean Corporation which is doing great things. I am leaving the city I love most for the mountains I love most in the state I love most.

There have been tears, of course; my own tears, and there were many nights of them and I am not ashamed of this. Pour your passion into anything for 23 years and one cannot simply flip a coin of decision and lie down in sweet slumber.

I yet have promises to keep.

I have been too small to meet all my obligations to my brothers, too big to settle for less than the attempt, and the sum is a sense of drowning in my own ego and a sea of need and inadequacy. Better anything, then, than posturing in exhaustion. Better anything than blindly following instinct and accolade. The choice is to take a deep breath and another look at that one life and the precious lives of one's family.

As one unsigned reader reminded me today, "The Charlotte Observer made you what you are and you are leaving. I suspect, anyway, that all your victories have been for purposes of giving yourself some kind of an image as a Messiah . . ."

The first part of that statement is true. The Observer gave me my chance and my forum unfettered. The second part chills me with a feeling of death if, somehow, it should contain the tiniest grain of truth. I think it is ridiculous but I do not know. I have been too busy to find out.

Another columnist recently ridiculed the young people who, by increasing numbers, are wasting their time and everybody else's by running around crying, "Who am I?" The columnist's conclusion: "That's an easy one to answer. They're bums!"

Yet I can understand, ridiculous as they might appear, why they ask the question of themselves. It is an important thing to know.

But there are no answers, really. There are only questions. All of us must keep asking the questions. When we stop asking and stop seeking we are in trouble.

This leads me to comment on the value of criticizing those things we love, including this city. It is necessary. It is the synthesis of growth—not only of cities and dollars but of man. To me, criticism and question is an essential of the Law of Love.

Come to think of it, the Law of Love has not been overly mentioned lately. Precedence has been given to Law and Order. There is, if you're willing to agonize about it a little, considerable difference between the two.

And as for the tears . . .

They seem to have dried and in their place have come jeers and sneers.

A tear and a jeer. There's a difference.

Examine, if you're willing to hurt more than somewhat, the dichotomy of that one.

I would like to escape morbidity in this last column, which is inevitable in commenting on the fears which rack this most bountiful of all lands of all time. I cannot escape it.

Many of us make a God of the painful reality of a historical moment and cry for a retreat from man's highest and noblest challenges.

Visionaries are scoffed at for their dreams.

There is good reason for this. Reality is what is left when the dreams are all burned out for lack of the fuel of faith and courage . . . and when the dreams are burned out the remainder is ashes.

So there. I've rambled and I haven't said much but the column is almost finished.

I am not taking leave of Holy Angels Nursery which, anyway, will be built because it must and by men and women and children for whom I have merely been the mouthpiece while they labored and sacrificed. Anyway, Carolina-Caribbean is giving Holy Angels a day each year of the take at "Tweetsie" and Beech Mountain. I am not taking leave of Boys Town.

Now. Purposely I have not allowed myself to think about nor to mention, a single name of colleagues here at The Observer or thousands of you in the Carolinas to whom I am in deep and unpayable debt.

You are . . . You have made my life and this column by giving me yours in one way or another and, because I cannot block out memories of most of you individually—the times, the places, the circumstances—the tears are beginning to roll.

So that's enough.

Never say Goodbye.

P.S.: To the lady who wrote asking that I return her copy of "Household Hints," some kind of book she sent to me three years ago . . .

May I buy you another?

October 6, 1968

Coming Home Again

The telephone rang five times before she answered. Not so long ago it would ring only twice. It takes a little longer since Dad died.

"Mama," I said, "I've decided to go back to The Observer."

"We-elll!" she crooned. It's her word, with a particular tone, to express complete approval. There was a short silence and then she added, "I think that's wise."

"Why?" I asked.

"You're middle-aged," she said. "I've always thought it's too cold in the mountains for middle-aged people."

So Mama was pleased and will subscribe to The Observer again. That's the way she always kept tabs on the family. First thing she would look for the column and if it was there she'd put the paper aside and go on with her chores, coming back to it later. If it was not there she would instantly call long distance and breathe jerkily until she learned that the grandchildren hadn't been run over or anything.

So Mama is pleased, if puzzled. She read the announcement in the paper. It is hard for her to understand why she keeps seeing "Kays Gary Is Back."

"Those people must be as forgetful as I am," she sighs. "They have said it already."

Mama, perhaps with a lot of company, doesn't understand promotion. It's another word for "pressure." The Typewriter and I stared at each other, silently, malevolently, for hours before we reached the conclusion that not even a tablet delivered to this space from Mount Olympus could fulfill the expectations of The Promotion.

So there has been some inside bleeding. Paralysis. Hysteria. It happens when you can't even go to the office Men's Room without seeing that huge orange and yellow billboard down the street—"Kays Gary Is Back."

So? It stops sometime soon and then, old man, there you are. The people are waiting. Do your thing.

Jim Bishop could have sounded smug when, in panic, I finally got him on a Friday phone. Even as I was leaving almost 30 months ago he was saying, "You'll be back." He wasn't smug. He was kind. "I know," he said. "I used to get the same feeling after taking a two-week vacation

. . . the feeling that I couldn't get out another column. But if you ever have it you don't lose it. Like riding a two-wheel bike. Even after 40 years you don't forget."

We talked about our fathers who aren't here, anymore, confessing insecurity because they aren't and we're the elders now and we talked about the elasticity of time and about bridging gaps. And we talked about bridging the gap one day between Charlotte and Hallandale, Florida. It was comforting.

The elasticity of time, two and one-half years. A father has died and so has a mountain-moving friend, and a grandchild has been born and another will be here in days. Two and one half years. People know a man named Spiro now. Suddenly, the world is topless. Or bottomless. Two and one half years and a raw and rugged mountain named Beech has become a lasting monument to leisure, chewing up and spitting out men on the way.

Two and one half years. There's a new Charlotte skyline. The sophomores are pros now and giggly girls are mothers. There are friendly, familiar faces and there are faces that should be here but aren't and I'm missing them. There are strange, young, new and intent faces and one wonders how long it'll take to bridge the gap if, indeed, it can be bridged.

Two and one half years and even at home, a new address, the column doesn't come.

"What," said Miss Boo, "are you thinking, just sitting there and staring?"

"I am listening," I said, "to a distant drum."

"Listen for the phone and doorbell instead," said she, "so I can take a bath."

No soul.

The letters are good and kind and sincere and appreciated though pressure-packed. Don't they know that almost all things are better in retrospect than in fact? Besides, the once-upon-a-time column leaned heavily on ideas from their letters.

EXAMPLE: The Promotion can't possibly use all letters and in the shuffle one of my favorites was omitted. It came from Bill Holland Jr. of Surfside Beach, S.C., and from the sound of it Bill must be the author of those 7-11 radio commercials.

"Two years ago," he wrote, "my mynah bird fell silent with your departure. As he sat on his perch in his cage, looked down and covered the article announcing your return he burst into beautiful song and so did I.''

Now that's soul!

Perhaps yet in some way the uptightness will give way to a few laughs, and anxious moments may turn into time for tenderness.

There must be adjustment.

At the moment, with Charlotte on Monday facing the most important decision of our lifetimes in the Charter vote, it matters little that Gary is back.

On the other hand, if Gary can outlast Morganna, doing her well-injunctioned thing, maybe The Promotion is not ALL bad.

Besides, we've just begun to bridge the gap, to pick up a common thread.

March 21, 1971

The Very End

Of the flashes of genius which strike students stymied by exam questions, we've just heard from an unsigned Monroe lad.

A science teacher popped the query: "Where does light go when you turn off a lamp in your room?"

A puzzled student finally scrawled: "It goes to the same place your lap goes when you stand up!"

And that's The Very End.

October 5, 1965

The everlasting bike giveaway—a behind-the-scenes shot in the Observer newsroom.

Bob Woods helps Kays with the Great Bike Giveaway, 1979.

Reporter at work.

A short-lived Beatles haircut, 1964.

Pumping gas for Vilonah Blake, 1979.

Contributions roll in for the Kennedy Memorial fund, 1964.

A contributor on the telephone, others waiting, 1964.

Learning to play the bagpipes, 1964. Major John Ward assists.

Would you be suspicious if this man offered you a free flower?

Old coins and foreign money for Holy Angels Nursery.

A big balloon parade for Boys' Town, 1968.

An investigation of gasoline giveaway cards, 1968.

Kays directs traffic during blackout, 1965.

Kays at his desk, 1968.

Susan McNeill helps Kays with his band uniform at a West Charlotte High School celebration. Band Director Richard Maxwell watches.

Reminiscences

Kays Gary's genius is his ability to make us feel. When he writes of the seasons of his youth, they become our own. When he painfully reveals his agonies at the death of his wife, Miss Boo, we grieve.

Kays moves us. He causes our hearts to show us what is true and important. He reassures us that in the things that count we are one with humankind.

Jerry Bledsoe

Spring Reigns

Rain.

Since Nov. 1, the Charlotte area has had two extra months of it, eight inches more than normal.

Rain.

To the farmer it is both a blessing and a curse.

To the bricklayer it is beans instead of beef at any price.

To a contractor it is a scalding wish that the job had been signed at cost-plus.

To a mother it is the premier test of patience and endurance.

To the salesman of rainwear and clothes dryers it is a bonus in any season.

To the Highway Patrol and hospital emergency rooms it is dreaded overtime.

To promoters of outdoor recreation it is a soggy black-jack.

To car-wash operators it is a marathon game of gin rummy.

To homeowners who built beside a sylvan stream it brings the question: "Why doesn't somebody do something about soil erosion?"

To homeowners with septic tanks it brings a wish for annexation and second thoughts about "the good old days."

But for the young:

To a boy it is sailing of chip ships down rivers of the mind to some reckless rendezvous beyond yon culvert.

It is building dams for tiny lakes.

It is squishing of mud between the toes just for the sight and feel of it, the spanking of feet into puddles just for the patterned splash of it.

To a young girl it is the poetic pattern of raindrops on a window with some soft, mysterious and romantic promise. It is lonely yet warm, wordless yet singing. And when your mother calls, "What are you doing?" it is the answer,

"Nothing" when you mean "Everything."
    Rain.

    To the old it is memories under a tin roof when the
drummer called a comforting tune while the rain barrels
filled.
    It was adventure in the attic with funny old clothes for
dress-up and pretend. It was love letters tied with a ribbon
that you shouldn't have undone but did and were puzzled
about and glad about.
    It was looking at old picture albums and laughing and
it was cracking black walnuts and hickory nuts on the
hearth and parching peanuts and popping corn in a wire
basket over the coals. It was pitching horse shoes in the
barn and finding hen's nests in the haymow and chasing
field mice in the corncrib and racing tobacco stick horses.
It was Mama at the after-supper organ and Papa reading
the Bible out loud and when it came your turn to give a
verse from memory you'd better not use "Jesus wept"
again.

    And to young lovers of any time and place the rain . . .
    Is sweetness, pure and clean to be walked in, with face
turned up and head bare, somehow defiant of any who may
wonder at your sanity because they don't have and don't
know about real baptism. The face, upturned, welcomes
heaven's kisses. And walking, just walking, is a celebration and prayer of thanks.
    And finally, when it is finished, rain brings on its
mightiest gift beginning with a rainbow . . .
    The explosion of green is upon us. The season of
growth and renewal has come with baptism.
    And all God's creatures know about that . . .
    Save one.
    And we're trying.
    Aren't we?
                                            April 1, 1973

Summer: Time For Daydreams

Summertime and the living is lazy. The adrenals flow like swamp water. The corpuscles shoot craps. Snake eyes. The thermometer goes up. The eyelids slide down.

Daydreams are of summers that were.

Iceman Sam Stagg and his wagon drawn by old Nell. A team. He didn't have to drive her. A thousand sultry mornings of heading out of the ice and coal yard had built in an automatic pilot. Turn left on Harper Street. Down the hill and up the hill to Maple Avenue and left again. Stop at the Caldwells'. Skip the Harrises. Twenty clip-clops to the Bowles house with the iron gate. . . .

A card in the front screen door would announce the day's order. The four sides were labeled: 10 Lbs., 20 Lbs., 50 Lbs., 100 Lbs. The side turned to the top was the order. Sam would squint at the sign, pull back the canvas cover, chip out a block with a big pick, swing it onto his back with the big tongs and plod to the back porch or kitchen and the icebox.

Kids scampered in from all over, mainly shanties four blocks back, to snitch ice chips while Sam was gone. He didn't care, of course, but sneaking made the whole thing more fun and the cold, cold ice on a tar-blistering day was a heavenly treat.

The icebox itself? It was the kids' job to empty the drip pan daily. Some kids drilled a hole in the floor under the icebox to eliminate that problem. Some fathers didn't appreciate their ingenuity.

Summers that were.

Flying a June bug on a thread. Digging a hole to make a cave. Stumping toes. Damming the creek. Skinnydipping. Who had, or wanted, a bathing suit? Poking tar bubbles. Chewing tar. Making slingshots and shooting cans. Getting green apple bellyaches. Buying and sipping a Three-Center which wasn't a Coke but it was better than syrup pepsin. Syrup pepsin was what Mama gave you for the green apple bellyache.

Matching tobacco tags, shooting marbles, pickin' blackberries and poke "sallit," chewing pepper grass and sour grass, make-believing Lindbergh, Tom Mix, Lefty

Grove. Seining for minnows, building tree houses, running FROM girls. Matching tobacco tags. Shooting marbles.

Making slingshots from dogwood and old inner tubes. Shooting cans and missing rabbits. Pushing a lawn mower. Remember? Before they had engines? Reading books and Liberty magazine and Literary Digest and Grit and The Observer Junior inserted in The Sunday Charlotte Observer.

Selling Cloverine salve. Playing "Ain't No Bears Out Tonight" and getting kissed by a girl hiding in the same bush and spitting for two days. Trying, without luck, to get the crowd to play "Ain't No Bears Out Tonight" the very next Saturday.

Going to the drugstore on hottest days because there was a ceiling fan turning slowly and a big Lucky Strike poster picturing a young actress prettier than peach ice cream—Loretta Young.

Not liking church because Sunday britches were itchy and all the fans put in the pews by the funeral home were for adults. Playing cow pasture baseball, the site selection logical. You didn't have to bring the bases.

Summers that were. Dusty roads and cooling creeks. Keep an eye out for mad dogs and John Dillinger and check out the rumor that an Indian Medicine Show is really coming for a week to the lot beside Griff Bridges's blacksmith shop. It is. It IS. In August and free! Gonna cut a woman in two!

Summertime again and the living is lazy. The air conditioner hums. The ice cubes click in the refrigerator. A neighbor rides by on his lawn mower. The TV set blares in competition with the stereo and hot rock.

Young people skim past on bicycles, mopeds, motorbikes, cars, skateboards. Headed for the pool, Carowinds, the beach, lake, summer camp. Papa heads for the golf course, Mama for the tennis courts. Tonight the fish camp. Tomorrow the world.

Yet the corpuscles shoot craps and come up snake eyes.

Until the small grandson asks, "Paw-Paw, did you fight in the Civil War?"

That did it. Bring on the Geritol and the skateboard. After all, Loretta Young is coming out of retirement.

Summer is. One more time.

                                              June 19, 1977

At Fall Of Leaf
Come Memories

Everyone has his own memories of the season. Like the leaves they fall unbidden.

Somewhere between sleep and wakefulness they come.

Is the stove's belly red in the kitchen? That sound—plup-plup-plupplupplupplup. Coffee. The smell will be here soon.

From the frosted fields, hounds are bugling a rabbit to a morning chase, through the purpled turnip tops, along the fence rows and to the woods where leaves swirl down from hardwoods, laying a crunchy carpet.

Squirrels pause and freeze, unblinking, acorns clasped in tiny paws until, with sound of snapping twig, they are gone into the treetop caverns and the oak sprawls stripped down to her mistletoes.

And there would be possums and persimmons out there and jewels of the autumn vine—the scuppernong and muscadine—purple and gold and waiting to dribble juice down a small chapped chin and its triumphant grin.

Oh, yes! Except the bell. . . .

It is for school and hurry, now, into the uniform of Old Hickory overalls, denim shirt and sweater with elbow patches, shoes with glue-your-own soles and, proudly, the fleece-lined av-i-a-tor cap. Pray to God in heaven Mama won't make you change 'em for the corduroy knickers and the long lisle stockings with the lumpy ankles where the long-john legs have to be folded over.

Oh, yes! Grab your dinner bucket (In cities and up North, you would later learn, it was called a "lunch pail") and don't ask what is inside. There is the cold sweet tater, the big jam biscuits and—if it's Monday and the preacher didn't come to dinner—maybe a piece of meat left over.

And your mother will be saying sleeves are NOT for wiping noses, all evidence abundantly to the contrary, as you race for the road.

If you were blind you would know school because it is warmer than home and because of the smells of chalk, oiled floors, young-lady teachers and no wet dogs.

You would rather be down at the general store smelling new leather and listening to old men except when the bell tolled at 10 in the morning.

That is when the old men would stop telling stories and be quiet.

A 10 o'clock bell would be from the church and not the school and after it rang awhile it would toll the hour of a funeral. In a little town, truly, no one had to ask for whom the bell tolled. Even the hounds in the fields, it seemed, stopped baying.

School, invariably, would end for the day after you had learned to spell "Constantinople" and failed at figuring out how many apples the farmer had left after, from a bucket of 20 apples worth $1.21, he had sold 37 cents worth.

But outside, where cider mills were pouring juice, where pumpkins begged jack-o-lantern appraisal, where small tornadoes rose from field stubble on roaring wings, where corn shocks could convert you into an instant Indian, where sassafras roots waited to be found and dug, where walking in on a hog-killing would entitle you to a package of fresh sausage, where invitations to corn-shuckin' parties lay up every lane—outside was the place to be young at the end of a summer grown fat and old.

It would be at the end of a day like that, discovery at last with a mother's help in arithmetic, how many apples the farmer had left, and privileged to stay up and listen to the Lux Radio Theatre, that the last log would burn through in the fireplace, fall between the irons and send showers of sparks up the chimney. That was bedtime's signal.

The bed was like a warm cocoon or womb, yet yielding dreams with shadows and shapes upon the walls, of the Four Horsemen, of dragons to be slain, of Everests to be climbed. . . .

Somewhere between sleep and wakefulness there are these memories alive.

Then suddenly that bridge is crossed. The sound is a furnace fan. Instant coffee awaits. Instant lather is ready with a disposable razor for a beard grown grey overnight. The house is warm but the hearth is cold and shining.

No bells are ringing. No bells are tolling.

And all the old men, wherever they are, are quiet.

October 25, 1977

Winter: Cruel And Beautiful

For months we've been preparing for it and dreading it and expressing anxiety almost daily about it.

Now it is here. Almost. It will arrive officially at 6:10 Saturday morning (EST) and, if weather forecasters are correct, you may not even notice, what with dashing around in shirt sleeves for golf, tennis or last-minute Christmas shopping.

Winter.

It'll be here for a three-month stay and there's nothing we can do about it except hope that it may be merciful.

We've raided the savings accounts and loaded the credit cards for insulation, storm doors and windows, wood stoves and wood. Our heating oil bills, almost double those of little more than a year ago, keep climbing with no ceiling in sight. It'll take years of fuel savings to pay for the stoves.

With Christmas upon us, we have tried to shed anxiety and fear and bitterness and all of us were doing right well until we went out to buy a Christmas tree. The price of that tree, it turned out, would have bought a load of firewood.

Winter.

Time was when we could get lyrical about it. There is no quiet like that across the countryside when snow is falling, no beauty more stimulating than a world seemingly sown with diamonds as the sun catches snow and icicles on the trees. Young cheeks flush with excitement and chill, young eyes dance with anticipation and laughter echoes down streets and across hills in welcome to winter.

Winter.

It's a season for the young. Sledding, skiing, skating parties. Snowball fights. The warmth of home. The delight of hot chocolate. The smells from the kitchen stove. Christmas and girlfriends and boyfriends. Discovery of a poet's soul on a walk in the woods.

It's a season for the memories of youth, too; of a simpler time when home seemed safe and secure and predictable. It was a time when so little seemed to be so much. There are luxurious memories of oranges and stick candy, too, divided among brothers, sisters, cousins.

There are memories of the roaring fire on the hearth with chestnuts in the coals and late-night corn poppings and the almost sensuous pleasure of a bed warmed by a flatiron or a hot water bottle wrapped in flannel, of learning how to use your hands to make shadow figures on the wall.

Memories bring back the sound of hounds baying in pursuit of rabbits on a crackling dawn, of tales told 'round the pot-bellied stove in the crossroads store, of waking to smells of perking coffee and frying strips of "streaked lean," of dashing down cold stairs to dress beside the kitchen stove.

At some point, alas, we lose our youth and, at times, our memories of it. Winter becomes a dread symbol of the dead or dying and of fear. Winter becomes a threat to life and health and security. We allow age to rob us of anticipation and adventure. Aching and swollen joints blot out memories.

Winter becomes a time of waiting and the waiting is for one more spring when life is renewed and its eternity affirmed.

We would have winter mean more than that; more than a time of waiting and of fear.

Winter's beauty is changeless if we are not. It is still a caring time and a sharing time and a time of striving and seeking. It is a time to be used instead of forfeiture to fear.

The birds need us as in no other season. So do the neighbors. So do the children.

Bejeweled mornings are ahead and winter's prayers wait to be said in gratitude for yesterdays and the promise of tomorrows.

And maybe, just maybe, on an ice-sheathed day when the wind slashes with its worst wintry blasts, we can laugh again as once we laughed and find a way to make some memories for the young.

December 21, 1979

Front Porches

Nobody builds front porches anymore, and I think the Communists are behind this.

That must have been old Joe Stalin's last major assault on The American Way, and he sure struck a blow.

They quit building porches on houses in about 1950 and by 1953 when Old Joe died very few people were sitting on the porches that were left.

Now the builders say the Communists haven't got a thing to do with it.

They say that people quit building front porches to save money, because of a desire for privacy and laziness, because of now-available air-conditioned comfort inside, because of set-back lines leaving houses too far from the street and because of the drift from downtown living where there's activity to watch from a porch.

Now this is just a round-about way of skirting the brass tacks fact that somebody put 'em up to it.

And that is just what Old Joe wanted. Oh, he was a smart one, all right.

I can see him sitting up there in the Kremlin chewing on his mustache and trying to think up some way to break up America, which would mean breaking up the community, which would mean breaking up the family.

"Dadgumovitch," he growled to his secretary, "I'm done thunk out, Comrade Dishova. What in the Helsinki we gonna do? Ain't you got no idears?"

And Comrade Dishova, who is scratching herself while reading a 1936 copy of The Saturday Evening Post, hands him the magazine so she can scratch with both hands.

"Here, oh, Peasant Cock O' The Walk" says she, "lookit this here capitalistic rag and maybe you'll think up sump'n 'nother."

Old Joe thumbs through the magazine, stops, studies one page long and hard and leaps to his feet.

"Wowski! Hotdogovitch!" he yells. "I done got it!"

His hands, trembling with excitement, rip out a Norman Rockwell picture of Maple Avenue, Centerville, U.S.A., showing a typical residential street scene.

Mamas and Papas and Grandmas are sitting on front porches.

Teen-age sweethearts are sitting in swings.

Kids are playing on the sidewalks all up and down the street in front of the porches.

A fat man is helping a skinny neighbor fix his lawnmower.

People on the porches are waving to sidewalk strollers and people passing in automobiles.

In the foreground a lady carrying a chocolate cake is handing it over to a front porch family and you get the idea that soon there'll be lemonade and an informal party as a part of daily life on The Street.

"The front porchski!" growls Old Joe. "Get ridda them things and we'll bust up The American Way."

So he called the Central Committee into all-night session and they hashed over the idea in detail.

Obviously the Americans were all a big family.

Everywhere else in the world people built walls or fences around the houses and the point was privacy, divorce from involvement with whatever went on next door.

Unlike any other people these Americans built porches not 30 feet from the street so they could see and be seen by everybody. Everybody had a bad habit of being involved with everybody and everything on the street—joys and sorrows, triumphs and failures.

Obviously, too, the porch held the family together, so the Central Committee decided on a tactic.

Create the desire for privacy, for backyard patios. Make 'em status symbols. Make Americans want to get behind hedges and fences, away from meddlesome neighbors. Talk about the value of the building dollar and ways to stretch it by eliminating—porches.

Then Grandma can go to the Old Folks Home. With no swings for evening courtin' watch young lovers hit the road.

Get rid of the porches, in short, and create a community of suspect strangers who are up to no-telling-what behind the house on a patio sheltered by fast-growing vines.

Divide, by gumski, and conquer and build boulevards for ghosts so that men fear to walk their own streets.

Well, it took 'em 15 years but they did it. The American Scene remains in scattered small towns and in isolated city areas like Charlotte's Dilworth.

The builders say they haven't had a request in years to build a porch. They figure the desire for porches disappeared for the same reasons other styles disappeared.

Poor fellows.

They just don't realize that it had to be a Communist plot.

August 29, 1965

Forty Years Ago

Affluence is one problem afflicting the Scouting program, said Gene Grimes as we munched barbecue sandwiches and talked to keep from counting calories.

Grimes, longtime Scout executive, was saying that one of Scouting's main objectives is to teach self-reliance and in affluent times young people don't have much need of it. Parental affluence and a full social life also makes leader-recruitment tough.

That took us into recollections of differences in then and now, the times when we were boys vs. the scene for today's young—recollections one dare not bore kids with today and their reaction is understandable. It's a different world.

"Remember," said Gene, "when you used to get punished by being sent to your room? Today, what's the point? He's got a radio back there, maybe his own TV, a record player, sometimes a telephone. That's punishment?

There's little motivation to learn how to build a raft if the kid or one of his friends has a motorboat, plus skis, plus a car to haul 'em to the lake. And what's with making Hunter's stew when there's a pizza place, a MacDonald's or Hardee's within hiking or Honda distance?

But it isn't just kids who are different. So are parents. Forty years ago how many of them each had a car? How many of them played golf, went to cocktail parties, weekended at mountains or beaches in second homes, took trips in campers?

The conversation wandered to tagging random recollections of 40 years ago.

The term "jet" was an adjective for black.

Nobody had heard of penicillin, sulfas or mycins.

Pneumonia meant you were halfway to the funeral home.

Nobody had heard of the A-Bomb, computers, Master Charge or TV. Supermarkets were just being introduced but a "chain store" was regarded as something subversive. The terms "integration" and "segregation" were academic, used only in the sciences.

For the young, "grass" was something you chopped out of cotton. A guitar was something only hillbillies and

Spaniards played. Any female who wore mascara or eye-shadow was a you-know-what. Movies didn't have ratings, though the Hayes office made sure that no actress ever exposed the "inner thigh." Motels were yet to become popular. Their forerunner, tourist cabins, had questionable reputations. The dime was the coin of the realm for the young. It would buy two of almost anything—gum drinks, popcorn, hot dogs and would play a nickelodeon (juke box) twice. Any teenage girl would have slashed her wrists before wearing jeans to school.

Any boy would have done the same rather than fight his way to school because his hair was over his ears. There were no under-20 entertainers except in movies. If you were lucky enough to take a trip with your parents to the beach you brought some of the ocean back in a bottle to prove it.

The only "uppers" and "downers" were on the Ferris Wheel and Merry-Go-Round once a year at the County Fair. If you ever got to drive a car it was on Saturday night when Pop and Mom stayed home. There were no drive-in movies. Self-starters were now standard equipment but there was a crank just in case. Some dreamer promised automatic transmissions being introduced with the Reo Flying Cloud. The car had no radio but some of them had four-note horns and all came with tire patching kits and running board.

Away from home there was one resource for the single person—a boarding house. No apartment complexes with color TV, pool and saunas, tennis courts and putting greens. You were making it if your room had hot and cold running water. A private bath? Who were you, Rockefeller?

If Charlotte had busy intersections it had to be Trade and Tryon and Tryon and Morehead. There were no shopping centers. North Carolina's Seventh Wonder was the state's only four-lane highway—Wilkinson Boulevard to the river. Our only tall buildings were Liberty Life (Baugh) and the Johnston Bldg. Neighborhood banks were yet to come. Stock car racing was an outlaw sport in the mountains. Moneyed ladies got a "perm" every fall and a finger wave every month. Golf was only at country clubs. Same for swimming pools. Campers and mobile homes hadn't been invented.

We were yet to experience air conditioners, power mowers, chain saws, portable radios, hair dryers, stereos, styling combs, deodorants, Disneyland, and synthetic fabrics besides rayon. Nylon might have been the name of

the ambassador from Finland. The biggest giveaway promotion was a set of dishes at the Thursday night movies. A
long distance phone call meant that daughter had eloped or
somebody had died. If there was a dog in the house you
could also look for pigs and chickens. If anything cost as
much as a dollar you got it for Christmas or not at all. Rock
and roll was a rock and a roll. You threw one and ate the
other . . .

Forty years ago.

                                              May 23, 1973

Attic Sales

I'm no good at attic sales. I want to buy everything. Almost everything. I'm no good as an attic salesman because most stuff I don't want to see go.

There was a triple-header attic sale Thursday and Friday next door. The Beautiful Bride was a part of it. They did well. But I . . .

There were those old "Yank" magazines you remember years ago. Artistically, technically, it was good. But there was no longer any place for it and it made sense for someone else to have it and appreciate it. Except I couldn't think like that. It would be worth $15-$20-$35 at an artist's sidewalk sale. But there's more to worth than a price tag. This had been a gift of a part of a person. True, if I kept it, it would be packed away still. I felt a chill when I saw the price the girls had marked on it. But I felt something else when, near the end of the sale, it was still there. Nobody wanted it. The price? Twenty-five cents.

Some things have a claim on blood and bone.

Like my father's old briefcase.

He's had several briefcases. This one had been the cheapest but the one he'd used most as a school principal for 35 years. It was worn at the corners. He had inked his name inside. I saw it when a lady started to pay for it then said: "I thought this was 25 cents instead of $1.25. It isn't worth that." She put it back, thank God. The B. B. saw my face, I guess, and put it away.

There were those old "Yank" magazines you remember if you were overseas in World War II and lived for "Sad Sack" and the pin-ups of Betty Grable and somebody named Sally Neal. They're collectors' items. They'd been buried for years, moved countless times. They were brittle. There was never time to re-read them. But they were always someplace like your Mama is always there someplace when you're a kid. And when another grey-haired man with a paunch bought them all there was a weakness in the knees. But he had been in the South Pacific in the time that was. Maybe he would read them, keep them. I achingly hope so.

Our family has dishes on top of dishes. Mama's and grandma's best and second best have been handed down to our children. But then there were a dozen others. . . .

They hadn't cost much. They couldn't have 50 years
ago because we didn't have much except each other at the
time. But they were the dishes I remember most because
they were the ones most used as we ate at the kitchen table
beside a window with a view of the backyard, an apple tree,
the iron wash pot, the barn and the "TEE-ARE." Other
people had other names for the "Tee-Are" but my parents
taught me that the other names were not for me to use.
"Tee-Are" was correct. I was almost grown before I knew
that "Tee-Are" wasn't a word but "T.R.," an abbreviation
for "Toilet Room" which was a pretty fancy name for our
two-holer.

Well, the rambling thoughts consume the mind as one
contemplates what was and is no more.

Those plain, cheap plates . . . Plain except for a tiny
figured border, worn in places where my fingers secretly
pushed black-eyed peas onto my fork—secretly because
early on I was taught, with the aid of wrist slaps, that one
keeps his hands out of the food.

$1.50. That's what they were priced for the lot. Nobody
bought them. Providence was being kind.

There was a time in the beginning of the attic sale
that I purposely hardened myself. We had to get rid of
junk. The B. B. was parting with things that had been a
part of her in another life when two married kids left the
mountains for New Jersey with high hopes and little else.
But she wasn't saying or revealing her feelings and so I
tried to measure up.

There was The Charlotte Observer with the giant
headline just over 29 years old. It read: PEACE. IT'S OVER.
Actually, it wasn't the world's best headline for the occasion. Civilization's biggest war was ended. Peace had come.

There was the "Time" magazine with the picture of a
vice-president who had just become President of the United
States on the cover—Harry Truman.

"Go ahead," I said. "Sell them."

"You don't have to," the B. B. said.

"I've never done anything with them," I said. "I probably never will," knowing that this was true.

My Beautiful Bride is something special.

When I asked, trying to be casual, how much they sold
for she said: "I never put them on sale. I put them away."

It isn't just things with my own memories involved
that rip me up in attic sales.

There are dolls with arms off, tricycles, pull toys with

wheels off, Pop Warner football uniforms, Cub Scout uniforms and too quickly the mind pictures the babies who aren't babies anymore. One would dam the curse of sentimentality but, failing, simply and silently damns it.

No more attic sales for me with those high chairs and rocking chairs.

There's just one attic sale item that helps offset a sense of loss when it is sold. I love to see lawnmowers sold at any price.

I hate lawnmowers.

November 10, 1974

Loving Trash

There's a mountain to be moved.

It's a paper mountain atop my desk with ragged, paper-clipped peaks, yellowed valleys and curling pink slips cascading down to the edges of an overflowing ashtray.

My desk. Scorpio's shrine, Capricorn's nightmare and it was ever thus. But once each year comes resolve with delivery of the new desk calendars.

Last year I struggled for hours to clean it. It was, to be sure, an emotional struggle because when it was done my priority pile of papers had simply been shifted from the left to the right side of the desk and the "things to remember" pile had been spread in a leftward leaning semicircle.

Ultimately, challenged by the do-it-now command of the new calendar, I finally scrapped it and decided to use 1976 all over again. With minor mental computations, I figured, it would serve another year and it did. True, on some occasions I was a day late for appointments, but all in all things worked out pretty much as always. True, also, I was one of the few to miss 1977 altogether but gained the distinction of living 1976 twice. I am told, by the news in review, there was not a lot of difference.

But now here we are again, a new desk calendar waiting and a mountain to be moved, at least shifted, again, and the first item I pick up is a Christmas card which reads: "All We Need Is Love!"

Strange it never had the impact on Dec. 20 it suddenly acquired on Dec. 26. The immediate day-after reaction is, "So what are we going to do with all this Christmas stuff?"

Well, what we will do with it is to exchange it for something else or wear it or play with it for awhile until we get bored with it or it goes out of style which may be next week or the week after that.

Love, on the other hand . . .

There seems to be so little time for it.

Things get in the way. We have to buy them or trade them or sell them and create a want for them at which point they become a necessity.

We have to get wide lapels and throw them away for narrow lapels or vice versa. If the hems are down they have to go up or in the middle or some place except where they are. We have to figure a way to make denim as dear as silk, beads and scarves as indispensable as bread and meat, something in sex that nobody ever knew before. If we can just afford that right thing on wheels or the thing with the right label or the things that will be better than the things most others have. . . .

WELL!

Then, by all that's holy, we will at last explore the dimensions of love.

And that is why I cannot clean my desk.

These mountains of papers all tell me, in one way or another, that love is alive in the human heart.

They are letters that have come all year long from people telling me about other people who are quiet royalty in the business of loving.

They tell me of individuals and neighborhood groups, heroic in small ways in dispensing love and concern.

They tell me about their laugh-a-minute Aunt Hattie, their Uncle Ben and his six toes or the antics of their children.

They are letters in response to needs of others. They are letters expressing thanks, even praise for a job I am paid to do.

All these papers, individually, have been free admission tickets to the greatest show on earth—the human family. Individually, they represent gifts of time for intimate sharing. Individually, they carry 13-cent stamps from somebody's earnings. And they have not yet received an adequate reply.

To anybody else my desk is heaped with trash. To me it is heaped with little bits of people and to sweep them into the can would be total rejection.

So I have moved them around a little. I have puffed away some dust. I have even installed a new 1978 desk calendar. It's easy to find. It's right under the Christmas card with the legend, "All We Need Is Love."

December 27, 1977

Pumping Gas

Nobody punched me in the nose or even cussed me but I got fired my first day on the job as a gas station attendant just because I was late. Reason: A pre-dawn traffic jam of gas-seekers, three miles long on Albemarle Road.

I lined up the job Thursday night at Jimmy Huntley's Exxon station at the Albemarle-Sharon Amity intersection. The gas pumps were closed and my tank had maybe a gallon left in it.

"Jimmy," I said, "I'll work for free Friday morning so I can see what things are like from your side of the pump."

"What you really want," said Jimmy with a weary grin," is a tank full of gas and this is the angle. Well, by golly, it's a new story and I thought I'd heard them all. Okay be here at 7:15 a.m."

I was up at 6:45 and on my way at 7:10 because the gas station is only 2½ miles and five minutes away.

In the Friday morning darkness it was still 2½ miles but it was 45 minutes away because Albemarle Road was jammed, traffic backed up beyond the entrance to Lake Forest. It took me 10 minutes just to get onto Albemarle. Another 35 minutes and I was still a block from the station, found a vacant lot, parked and walked the rest of the way.

"Where you been?" Jimmy shouted. "Start pumpin'!"

Five of us manned six pumps. $3 limit.

Jimmy jammed a wad of one dollar bills in my coverall pocket.

"I've been in that line two hours," sighed a young, sleepy-eyed redhead in a red Toyota. "Boy, I can't believe I'm actually getting gas." The smile never left her face.

Nobody was picky about whether they got regular, Plus or Extra. High octane went into VWs and regular into Buicks.

"I never seen anything like it," mumbled a middle-aged woman in a station wagon. "Is it true there'll be no gas at all next week anywhere?" I told her nobody knew from anything. I hoped it was a rumor.

There was no dallying. Pump it fast, get the three bucks while it's pumping and move'er.

"I've never seen so many strangers in my life," said Jimmy Huntley. "You wonder where on earth they bought gas before. I had a heavy business anyway, knew 'em all by name. Seventy five per cent of these people I never saw in my life."

A novice gas pumper wishes the auto industry would standardize gas caps and tank necks. They're situated in the back, on both sides, in front and under the hood. And a pump attendant could cuss when the driver of a car with a locked tank cap hands over a bunch of 50 keys and doesn't know which one fits.

There was a woman with another car at home. Could she come back with it?

"If you get in line at 6 o'clock tomorrow morning and get to the tank by 9," I told her.

Nine a.m. would be the cut-off point, Jimmy said, because 1,200 gallons a day is the most he could pump and have a little five days a week. He'd started at 7. He'd pump 1,200 gallons in two hours.

Only one man held up the pump action for several minutes. He was walking around saying there really isn't a fuel shortage. Jimmy politely asked him to quickly move out. He did.

"Lord," Jimmy said, "it's 10 til 9 and I'd rather take a dose of salts than go out and close the entrance.

On Albemarle and Sharon-Amity, both with entrances to Huntley's station, lines of cars were backed up as far as I could see.

"I'll do it," I said.

"Don't cut off that Day-Care Center bus," he said. "Those little kids . . . Cut it off behind the bus."

I put the "Last Car" sign on the back of the bus. The driver of the next car back threw up his hands, started driving in, anyway.

"I got to," he said. "I'm empty right here. I can't get another block."

Jimmy let him in. He was empty.

The next car tried to swing in, too.

I refused him. He rolled up his window, pounded his steering wheel. He was spitting mad but he drove on saying things I couldn't hear.

I never got to see the cheaters. Every car needed the $3 worth. There were only two that $3 filled the tank.

To include the day-care bus we had to let cars in front of it, come in as well. We pumped 1,500 instead of 1,200 gallons. That would mean 300 fewer gallons the next day.

In two hours nobody had time to answer two constantly ringing phones. The first, at 9:15, was a lady who wanted to know if she hurried down could she get 10 gallons. And the next and the next and the next would be emergencies, real or conned. That's the way Jimmy Huntley would spend the next 22 hours.

"Lord," he said again, "I'd rather take a dose of salts. I wish this was Indianapolis."

Indiana has no problem. Hasn't had. No lines, no limits. Yet, last week its application for additional allocation was approved. North Carolina's was turned down. Somebody in Washington loves Indiana.

"Do I get my gas?" I asked.

Jimmy laughed. "This one time then it's take your place in line because you're fired. . . . A man who can't get to work on time."

It was worth it.

"Ain't I seen you on TV?" my last customer asked.

"You might," I said. "Me and the mayor. Who else in Charlotte has a full tank of gas?"

February 24, 1974

"Good Morning, Miss Boo!"

Dear . . .

You wrote, without ever really knowing it, many of these columns for a lot of years, in good times and bad, and so you must know how tough it is to write this one.

You wrote much of the last one only two days before and you liked it and told me so, especially the parts which said, "Love is living when all else is gone" and "Love is a promise of a new beginning when the end has already come."

Those lines leapt from the typewriter so easily.

But now . . .

Nights have been filled with silent screams and the marching of armies of guilt through the deepest entrenchments of Being . . .

And yet . . .

You would smile, now, reproachfully, at the disillusionments I've held so recently—that people have changed, that negativism is abroad in the land, that people no longer care about the mattermost.

You can smile because now you know.

It isn't just the thoughtful notes and letters from people the world acclaims as great—the governors, the senators, the judges, the venerable and proven wise men.

You can smile because the people we thought of as friends have loomed larger than life itself. And so have the people we didn't really know but cared. Dear God, you wouldn't believe how they cared about you . . . how much they really knew!

They knew and know, so many of them, that while Kays was taking the bows that there was someone else there in the shadows refusing to blow the whistle on his weaknesses and failures.

Your people that not even I knew but who remembered when:

"She was the only person who ever helped me in time of need. . . ."

And this one from Sallie Hulak, who worked for you when you were head of Charity Hospitalization and then a supervisor of the Welfare Department:

"Those of us who knew her in high school and then were fortunate enough to have her as a boss will never forget her beautiful character. She had a rare and natural beauty and in my entire business career she stands above all other bosses by her strong, human approach to those of us under her direction. She made us LOVE to work hard She was . . .''

And the doctors wrote. Some of them are old, now, and their handwriting was shaky but they remembered someone more than a patient and one of them even penned to me, ''If only there were some way I could relieve your suffering!''

And the housewives wrote and the young people wrote and the ministers and salesmen and the tradesmen and your appliance repairman. Not just cards. They WROTE by the hundreds and with a depth of feeling and love I could never match.

Dear . . .

They're planting trees for you in Israel. You are being memorialized by support of children in Israel's B'nai B'rith Children's Home. Catholics are celebrating special Masses for you and they and Jewish people and others of all faiths have sent scores of memorials to the Baptist Orphanage, Mills Home, Thomasville, where your beloved mother and father were reared, worked and died.

Your memory is being perpetuated at Holy Angels Nursery, Boys Town, High Point College, Lees McRae College, the Winston-Salem Foundation, American Cancer Society, Tuberculosis Association, Central Piedmont Community College. And on. And on.

I was wrong about the people, dear, as I have been wrong about so many things that only you really knew.

And so, even in the nights with the silent screams, we're trying. You'd be proud of Debbie. And of Sadie who won't go somewhere else even for more money. They're trying very hard to make a home of an apartment. But when they wind your music box, the one with the dancing little clowns . . . And when they play the allegro from Tschiakovsky's Concerto in C Minor . . . You'd be proud of Bill and the home he's making for Ann and little Billy and Lori who looks so much like you.

All those years. So many memories. Happy years. And then too many with pain, an unbelievable series of afflictions. Job had nothing on you. And we kept saying there'd be a better day. The symbol was that silly little train that tooted and blew smoke and carried two helium balloons, one fore and one aft, with the printed words: ''Boo-Kays

Special . . . It Never Stops." You liked that. You even laughed and cried at the same time when you'd pull the switch and let 'er run. You hadn't pulled the switch in a long time. I wish you had because I've got news for you . . .

It still runs and the whistle isn't mournful at all.

There is one thing above all that my memory clings to.

It is the wreck in 1941 near Newton. You were just 19. We had just fallen in love but I wasn't with you then, either. One person died. You were to be the second but there was a man—a Dr. Frank Jones. And somehow, after weeks and months, he and God gave you life. Thirty more years of life. And in those thirty years two fine children, two super-grandchildren and countless people who rejoiced that you were here.

And so now I'll tell you something I have told you before.

Never say "goodby." Or even "good night."

Over and over I'm going to keep saying:

"Love is living when all else is gone."

And one more thing, for night has ended . . .

"Good morning, Miss Boo!"

August 1, 1971

[Alice Brett Howell Gary, "Miss Boo," died July 17, 1971]

Pat Hall

Pat Hall, 57, is dead, and the shock is felt through a city and a state where he made things happen.

There was no surprise, though, for the poor kid who grew up in Oakhurst to become a dreamer, promoter and master developer.

Some weeks ago, in a moment of attempted levity, he showed a friend his design of his own casket. Nobody laughed, and Pat loved laughter. Everyone who knew him has a story. Mine is the memory of the time he put me in the doghouse at home for days.

Years ago Pat invited friends by the hundreds to come to his Arrowood property on a December weekend to choose and cut their own Christmas trees. It was a party always. A big party.

My wife and I were late for the party one year. Most of the people had gone. Entertainment had included giving families helicopter rides. But with Pat no party could end when two or more were gathered. He told my wife she'd see me later and insisted I take a helicopter ride with him.

You could not resist Pat anymore than you could resist a bulldozer, and in minutes I was in the helicopter. Next came Pat and a pig—a real-live pig with a red bow around its neck. Before I could protest, the pig was in my lap, Pat was beside the pilot, and we were airborne and squealing. Pat claimed I was doing the squealing and blaming the pig.

Only minutes aloft we were in darkness, with the lighted city sprawling beneath us. Pat was directing the pilot to fly north over the just-abandoned Nike missile plant, and it was there he unfolded his plan for its development into a massive warehouse complex.

With it, his monologue had Charlotte growing like Los Angeles. It bothered him little the helicopter was making so much racket and the pig and I were so panic-stricken we couldn't appreciate another of his orations on Charlotte —horizons unlimited.

Finally, with some insistence on the pilot's part, Pat decided there was no use returning to Arrowood. Friends had borrowed his river house for the weekend. There were floodlights there. The helicopter would take us to Lake Wylie.

There, Pat and the pig and I joined the party while the

pilot quietly disappeared. It was close to 4 a.m. when I got home, and it was some days before a note from Pat got me out of the doghouse. The note convinced her it was not easy for old friends to leave a Pat Hall party.

Some of him was a little boy, an industrial age Tom Sawyer or certainly Horatio Alger hero. His Tinker Toys, though, involved whole construction firms and giant acreages and thousands of jobs.

Most recently, as head of the Housing Authority, his dreams had been just as daring for housing for the elderly in downtown Charlotte.

Yes, we'll miss Pat Hall.

Nobody ever again is likely to take me in a Rolls-Royce to a drive-in for a hamburger, and laughter will never be so easy.

November 10, 1978

Tom Black

Tom F. Black sold his dairy, barn and all, a handful of years ago but he still walks over the property and visits the new tenants almost every day.

The new tenants, he vows, are a darned sight prettier than the Jerseys and Guernseys that once roamed the place. There are girls, hundreds of them, "and I've still got good eyes."

The new barn is something else, too. It's the sleek, modern Eastern Air Lines reservations and computer complex at Park Road and Fairview.

All the bustle, the flashing lights on control panels, the spinning computers, are magnificently ignored by Mr. Black. His puckish face wreathed in smiles, he wanders up and down the rows of girls as they take calls from 32 cities. Greetings, small talk, friendly pats from Mr. Black take priority.

Tuesday afternoon with Mrs. Black, he walked "across the pasture" (now a huge, paved parking lot) for his usual visit. This time it wasn't so usual. EAL personnel chimed out with "Happy Birthday To You . . ." and 88 candles on a big cake burned brightly.

"Looks to me," he laughed, "like you're wastin' a mighty lot of time from work."

Happily munching the cake, he recalled days when as one of 12 children of a tenant farmer, he set out on his own, bought the 100 acres at Park and Fairview in 1907 for $30 an acre and "finally paid for it in seven years."

On being 88 years old he said, "It's the finest time of life."

If he were starting out again at age 20, today, what would he do to make a living?

"I believe," he said with a grin, "I just might get into real estate. It beats selling buttermilk."

The EAL crowd guffawed.

The land he'd bought in 1930 at $30 an acre has sold in recent years for $10,000 an acre and up.

An office building is rising next door and, Mr. Black said, "some people are pesterin' me about buying my house and the seven acres left."

Though there's scarcely enough room to graze a cow anymore, he indicated he'd hold on to his 100th birthday, at least, because "a man likes to stay on his home place."

September 14, 1965

Paul Samele

For all the people out there soaking up the sun there was no way to miss him.

It was something like a picture with a slow shifting of component parts so that the scene never really changed . . .

Except for him.

His was the one figure that kept darting while the thousands of others were in slow motion. Olive-skinned and lean, black curls screwed tightly to his head and neck, eyes flashing messages of energy frantic to be spent, he hurled himself into the surf shouting for attention. Dashing out of the water it was always to challenge some-body with a ball, a kite or a race to the dunes and back.

His nearest approach to a quiet moment was when the tides began to leave little pools and he attempted to build dams to trap tiny minnows before they could escape in the surf's lacy skirt. But even this was a feverish effort.

One would guess he was about 11, maybe 12, and a man in middle age would try to remember how it had been with him at age 12 if there ever had been a time. . . .

There was a wandering wisp of recollection, of being stunned at the sight of the sea, of being a bit fearful, of con-templating vastness of breadth and depth and darkness and eternity of motion.

There was that much, a sighing recollection of a 12-year-old's awareness of an infinitesimal self, a bare grain-of-a-grain in an endless beach of an awesomely ordered universe. Humility, one supposes, had been thus introduced to a 12-year-old boy from an inland village on his first visit to the sea.

But this one, distinctly from the city and a Yankee city at that, was experiencing none of this. Aggressive, daring, confident—he was all that until the sun dipped behind the dunes and suddenly almost everyone was gone. He stood, dripping and with hands on skinny hipbones, looking up the beach and down the beach and out to sea and then began to stomp heavy footprints in the sand.

Quickly the footprints washed away. He then found a stick and began to write in the sand. Standing back, surveying his work, he shook his head, walked up the beach and began to scratch out letters, larger and larger.

Finally, the letters stretched 50 yards in length and half the depth of the world's widest beach.

It was deep dusk when he stood on the dunes and watched the surf creep closer to his work. Listlessly, he flipped the stick and was gone.

The words scratched in the sand, big enough to be read from a miles-high aircraft, were: P-A-U-L S-A-M-E-L-E.

Paule Samele, New York City, had tried. One wondered at what it had done to him as, despite all his efforts, the universe had rejected his announcement of indelible identity.

There was no way to know because the beach was smooth the next morning and set with that slow-shifting scene of color and people. If Paul Samele was out there he had suddenly become much, much older.

May 11, 1973

Jake Houston

The king of Carolinas press photographers lies in a coma at Charlotte's Presbyterian Hospital, his life measured in the metronome-paced drip-drip-drip of intravenous fluids.

Last Tuesday's massive cerebral hemorrhage is the only thing John Thomas "Jake" Houston, 75, ever did quietly.

For most of the three decades reaching into the '50s, the Carolinas' first fulltime newspaper photographer lived and worked with flair and in sartorial splendor.

In the presence of presidents, nobles or steel-driving men, whether covering a football game, a strike or a socialite's wedding, he was an event himself, his own parade, an unforgettable character.

His walk was that of a pigeon-toed duck.

His speech was replete with confidently-delivered malapropisms.

He was nearly blind most of his professional life.

Yet he was a photographer without peer in an Observer career from 1929 through 1953.

Jake in a coma? One must believe it because he didn't take his old Speed Graphic camera along. He did years ago when hauled to the hospital for an emergency appendectomy, insisting that he be allowed to photograph his own surgery. Hospital authorities balked. Jake insisted. He won.

The picture was the thing at all costs.

He would walk the wings of airplanes to get shots of air shows, stomp his way past security people to get shots of presidents or other celebrities and, resplendent in his colorful toggery, find them stunned and cooperative with his manner.

Despite a White House announcement in the '30s that Vice President Henry Wallace would submit to no interviews during a mission to the South, it was Jake who clambered aboard his train with reporter Hal Tribble during a two-minute whistle-stop here and, loaded with equipment and jostling the dignitaries in the crowded cars, peered into each face searching for the vice president. Finally, in the dining car, he tapped the shoulder of a diner in a party of four and asked, "Hey, Bud, which one is

Wallace?''

The vice president, thus tapped, submitted. The picture of "Bud" was excellent. Jake sent him a copy.

"I don't guess," says retired, longtime Observer Staffer LeGette Blythe, there's any story we didn't cover in the '30s and '40s. Jake was the only photographer for years. We had President Roosevelt a couple of times and Truman once in the White House. Nobody and nothing intimidated Jake."

When Roosevelt posed formally during one session Jake implored, "Just try to look human!" breaking the president up.

His most memorable shot of Roosevelt came when, late on the assignment, Houston chased Roosevelt's train down the tracks. The president, seated on the observation platform with a cigarette holder in his mouth, leaned back and roared at the sight. Houston's one shot, taken on the run, went around the world.

Born in Columbia, reared in Camden, Jake spent almost four years studying art at the Pennsylvania Academy of Fine Arts. Later he said he'd been more interested in painting the town than in painting on canvas and left for Florida to get rich in the land boom of the '20s. His second day there he got a job with the St. Petersburg Times as an artist.

When the boom became a bust, "they told me to keep a job I'd have to do more, so they gave me a camera and made me a photographer and a pencil and told me to report."

Flash bulbs hadn't been invented. It was a day when flash powder in a pan was ignited to produce an explosion of light for pictures. Jake was photographing heavyweight boxing champ Jack Dempsey when an accidental explosion of the powder left him almost blind.

Doctors in Atlanta advised him that bright tropical sunlight would further cripple his eyes. Married to Margaret Peeler, an Atlanta native and cub reporter also on the Times, Jake applied for work with The Observer and began to build his legend.

A charter member of the National Press Photographers Association and president of the North Carolina Press Photographers Association, Jake's credentials extended across the board from spot news, to sports, features and fashion.

"I never understood it," said Dick Pitts, an Observer colleague now retired. "There were times he'd have me strike a match near the subject in order to focus properly but most times he just fired away out of instinct and the shots were sharp, superb.''

Once when national gridiron powers Duke and Pitt met during a heavy snowstorm in Duke Stadium, Jake alone got pictures reflecting the mood, scene and drama of the struggle and perhaps the greatest collegiate punting performance of all time by Duke's Eric Tipton.

Never did Jake use light meters, strobes, automatic focusing or motored cameras now essential in photography.

Despite urgings by his editors to let reporters do the interviewing, Jake couldn't resist, after long admiring a sports jacket worn by an English nobleman, cutting in with: ''Lord, I'd throw you down for that coat. What do you do for a livin'?''

An annual fixture at the prestigious Camden Cup races, Jake was also its sartorial star. ''The checks in his sports coats was so large,'' one colleague said, ''it took two ordinary sport coats to make one check in his.''

His malapropisms were similarly colorful.

He might innocently explain that he'd just taken a picture of a little girl bitten by a rattlesnake whose life had been saved ''by a tournament her father put on her arm,'' or that a picture of a wreck victim was upcoming of ''this lady lying prostitute on Wilkinson Boulevard.''

The day Jake left the newsroom in 1953, the first Saturday his sunburst sports jacket failed to dominate the sideline scene of football stadia and every Easter fashion parade since, things have seemed a bit more bland, a tad more routine. There seem to have been more sighs, fewer laughs, less anticipation.

Now we know what it was. He and his breed are gone.

Except for memory, the greening pastures have browned.

In recent years he has painted pictures, dabbled at gourmet cooking, jousted with his grandsons, welcomed a party, remained faithful to rainbowed threads.

Now he is quiet. He can't hear the ''thanks.''

Life is only in the small droplets now—drip, drip, drip.

But, hey Jake, to uncounted hundreds of thousands of us you made a happy and long-memoried difference!

February 5, 1978

Ella Walker

Oh, but you are wrong.

A contented woman does exist; a perfectly contented woman.

She has everything she wants.

Only tomorrow can be finer than today.

And Charlotte, quite literally, lies at her feet.

You'll find her at 513 S. Cecil St.

Her tiny house and its front porch at the corner of Baxter and Cecil is a placid little island in a metropolitan sea.

Five feet to the right of her porch is the wall of a new office building. Eight feet to the left is Baxter and two big office buildings on the other side.

Below and in front of her, like toys for the queen, lie Charlottetown Mall, Kings Drive, Independence Boulevard and the streams of cars.

Beyond these is a background, left to right, of Covenant's spire, Addison Apartments, the cluster of downtown towers.

"The finest view in Charlotte . . . the finest."

The soft voice, warm and streaked with pride, belongs to Mrs. Ella B. Walker, 85.

The alert light in her eyes sparks in contrast to the soft folds of her face as she says, "This is my never-movin' home and I've seen a heap of happenin' since I came to it."

She came to it in 1911, one proud child of Sam Kirkpatrick's 16 proud children out near Sardis.

"My daddy said he'd teach us how to work and hellfire if we'd steal and it was a big thing he gave us and when I married Silas Walker I married me a Kirkpatrick kind of man."

Silas Walker had built this house and the day they had moved in the last bill on it had been paid. Down below they worked the cotton and trapped the rabbit where now cars slide along concrete ribbons and thousands hurry in and out of sleek, cubed buildings.

"The world has done come in all around but I like it," Mrs. Walker says. "It keeps the lonesome away."

'The lonesome' came in 1932 when Silas Walker died.

"Killed hisself workin' jobs day and night but that was his way. And what we gave our children took."

Three daughters and two sons graduated from high

school, business school or college and "went up the road."
All have good jobs in New York, married "good men and
women."

"They pay all my bills, phone me every week, come to
see me or take me up there but, I don't like up there.
They're all kind of hemmed in like."

And in 1943 her sons made her quit her dollar-a-day
domestic work.

"I've had a hankering to get me some of this $5 and $6
a day pay but they got the doctor to back 'em up. I've got
my garden, anyway."

The garden looks like a doll's dream with its tiny
walks, precisely clipped edges and bricked flower bed
borders. But flowers bloom in profusion from March into
November. One postage stamp corner flourishes with
vegetables.

Every Saturday Mrs. Ella B. Walker goes "up the hill,
out Queens and all the way to Providence selling my
flowers."

"Bill and Tom take me there," she chuckles, pointing
to her feet. "A girl pushes my cart of flowers."

Some chide her for working, she says, "but they are
rent house people. I never lived in a rent house. Ain't going
to. They say I got plenty of money. Maybe I have and maybe
I haven't, but if I got it it's in the bank where it's s'posed to
be. 'Sides, work is my way. It's the Kirkpatrick-Walker
way."

She is amused at the curious stares she gets when
friends sometimes take her to the fashionable Charlotte
suburb which once was her father's farm.

"I don't tell 'em I'm looking at the place where the hog
pen and the chicken house and the barn was. They don't
know all that belonged to my daddy who got a good price."

She shudders to think what the 118 acres would be
worth today. "I could have a maid," she said with a laugh,
"and wouldn't that be a mess?"

Yes, there has been talk of business wanting her little
house and corner for $19,000, "but what am I goin' do
with $19,000? They ain't goin' to get it. Some say I ought to
move out to one of these fancy houses at the edge but I ain't
movin' to the thickets. No, sir. And I ain't moving to a
rented house. I got the world right here."

"My Silas planted this rose bush out in back. I've kept
it going bigger and prettier than ever these 33 years."

She turned the blossom over with her fingers, held it to

the sun. And then her hand waved, wand-like, at the city at
her feet.

"Everything is right here. Ain't it the truth?"

September 29, 1965

The Littl'uns

Every time we think of it we laugh until the tears roll.

And if God ever laughed it was during Wednesday night's high wind and rain storm.

Jerry Simpson, 5, lay abed with his papa while the wind screamed around their home on Rt. 2, Waxhaw. Finally came a quivering question:

"Daddy, what would we do if this tornado blew us away?"

"Why son," said daddy quietly, "We just trust in the Lord to take care of us!"

"Are you kiddin'?" shot back Jerry sitting bolt upright in bed. . . . "He's the one who MAKES these things!"

January 31, 1959

Cinderella
Stories

With compassion, sympathy and spiritual insight Kays Gary has used his great gift of words to play on the heart strings of his readers. He has touched the lives of many through his daily columns. In his writings there shines a beauty and optimism and kindliness that is so characteristic of Kays. This is especially true of all he has written about Holy Angels and Maria, to whom he refers as a Miracle of Love.

Kays Gary has been the true guardian Angel of Holy Angels Nursery from that first day when he came to visit me and then wrote the story of Maria in his Charlotte Observer column. He became a great advocate of the nursery when he first learned that I needed funds to build a new wing on the engineer's cottage which had been used for her day nursery and was later converted into a home for the birth-defected babies that came to me after Kays wrote the story about Maria.

To give his appeal for funds a national impact, Kays sought the influence of another great columnist. He wrote to Jim Bishop. Kays wrote him the story of Maria and Holy Angels, and the great need for that new wing. He told him of an idea of his for getting funds—an appeal for contributions of old coins and foreign currency to be auctioned for Holy Angels. He assured Jim that Holy Angels offered no daily miracles for these precious children, but what it did offer in abundance was LOVE and that "when the Sisters held these precious ones in their arms, that is when the angels sing" and Kays added, "Can you hear them, Jim?" Jim Bishop wrote, "No, I can't. One thing I know, my friend, you wrecked my day . . . now I have a head full of angels and Nuns who spend their days "nuzzling" leftovers and worrying about where they are going to get tomorrow's milk." At the end of that column Jim wrote to Kays, "If you think I am the type that will fall for your sob story, you're mistaken. Angels indeed!"

Ah, but Jim had fallen for it and that column of his in response to Kays' appeal and his suggestion about collecting old coins and foreign currency for auction for Holy Angels brought in $2,000 in one mail. Then in response to Jim's comment about his wrecked day, Kays wrote, "If my

letter about Holy Angels wrecked your day, then we are
even now. You wrecked my night. But beautifully
. . . Mother's Day ended with a nervous twitch when I
learned that your Holy Angels column appeared in the New
York Journal American Thursday afternoon, a full weekend ahead of all other papers—including our own. It was
10 p.m. when the twitch became unbearable. I tore out of
the office, grabbed the key to our post office box, opened it
and. . . . So you can't hear the Angels sing, hey? You're
spoofing. I heard them at that moment. They came in clear
and strong as I pawed through that river of mail . . . The
total, Jim Bishop? Two thousand dollars.''

Kays continued to bring the needs of Holy Angels to
the attention of his readers, and in time his idea of coins
for auction for Holy Angels brought more than $40,000.
And the Nursery got that new wing.

Before Kays took his leave of absence from the Charlotte Observer to join the Carolina Caribbean Corporation
in 1968, he wrote in his column, "I am not taking leave of
Holy Angels." This he proved by being instrumental in
having a benefit day at Tweetsie Railroad for Holy Angels.
On opening day in June 1969, Blowing Rock newspapers
announced that the historic little train would open its
season by huffing and puffing for Holy Angels. Tweetsie
tooted all day for the Nursery to the tune of $2,800.00.

Time and time again Kays has given us support by his
newspaper columns, his encouraging telephone calls and
by his friendly visits. He makes a special visit every year
on December 20, Maria's birthday. That is also the birthday of his daughter, Debbie, and when Debbie resided in
Charlotte, she brought added joy to Maria by coming with
Kays to Holy Angels for the double birthday party. And
then came the visit when Kays returned to Charlotte after
an absence of three years and 25 days. He wrote about this
visit with Maria and me in his November 7, 1971, column
in The Charlotte Observer. About the Nursery he wrote:

Holy Angels Nursery, a place like no other, a
singularly happy place where the littlest angels
sing and one can hear the lullaby, the requiem
and the anthem. A place like no other. A dispen-
sary of love. A bottomless reservoir of caring. A
temple of tenderness. A fortress against suffering. A sanctuary of souls of cherubs. An in-
cubator of liberation of innocents from cruelties
companion of births severest defects . . . A place

where all babies are beautiful . . . and Maria—
the miracle of love.

For all this and for countless other reasons, Kays is
truly the Guardian Angel of Holy Angels Nursery and its
great true friend.

Sister Marie Patrice
Administrator,
Holy Angels Nursery

Angels Sang Lullabies

They brought it to her when it was three weeks old.

It was, they said, a hydrocephalic "vegetable."

It would live no longer than six months, would never be able to lift its huge head and would never emit more than a crying sound.

Where its back should have been was a huge tumor.

There were two appendages which, if they had not been twisted or paralyzed, would have been legs.

"Please," said the doctor, "take it!"

He did not have to say "Please!" to Sister Patrice.

Her soft brown eyes saw only a loveless baby. Her soft fingers touched as only a baby is touched.

And the angels must have hovered over Belmont's Sacred Heart that day to hum a lullaby.

That was almost four years ago.

And there were endless nights when Sister Patrice implored the angels to hum a little louder so that she could hear them, too.

Sister Patrice had the Day Nursery for babies from four weeks to five years old—as many as 52 at a time for 12 years now.

But she had This One, too.

And while she fondled the misshapen body for hours on end, fed it with an eye-dropper and held it close through the nights, its old sound was the anguished cry of the little animal.

The days were like this, too—days that became weeks and weeks that became months beyond the allotted six.

Even doctors can be amazed. Sister Patrice and her colleagues had but one thing to give the doomed child but this they gave, gave and constantly. This One was not left to lie crying in its crib.

Then there was a day. Sister Patrice held This One on her lap. It lay there with its head on her knees while she massaged the neck and crooned her songs. Suddenly This One smiled! Then came a gurgling noise.

"I almost dropped her!" Sister said. "She did it again.

All the Sisters were so happy!''

And on this day she, too, heard the angels sing.

Doctors can be amazed. And they, too, can find hope.

They operated on the back. With the tumor gone, they said, the head would increase in size. It would bring more pain.

But it didn't. The head began to shrink. It receded nine inches to almost normal. And This One, named Maria, began to gurgle more and more. And now, when she smiled, everybody—not just Sister Patrice—saw the flashing dimples, the blue eyes, the shining brown-gold hair, the head held high.

Now? Maria talks as well as most four-year-olds. She can spin her wheelchair on a dime. She wheels it to the piano and picks out a tune note by note.

"And later there'll be operations on her legs and feet and one day she may walk with braces and crutches," says Sister Patrice. "And she'll go to high school and college and . . . oh, she's a lovely, bright one!"

Nobody argues.

The word of Maria and Sister Patrice got around. Others wanted her to take their hopeless and helpless babies. A few she could take. But there was no room.

And so she asked the Sisters of Sacred Heart to borrow money to build a nursing home, but they could not until a debt on the college was paid.

Then she asked for, and got, their permission to solicit.

She visited three men in Gastonia. She should not, they told her, be out soliciting. She had the Day Nursery to run. They suggested formation of a board of directors.

"Good," she said, "you are members."

There is no organization yet. But the foundations of a $40,000 building were being poured to care for 12 crib cases up to six years old.. Sister Patrice was supervising. Little Maria watched and waved from a window.

Where is the money coming from?

Sister Patrice does not know.

She just knows how to love babies.

January 6, 1960

Jim Bishop

Jim Bishop
780 Ocean Ave.
Sea Bright, N.J.
Dear Jim:

If my letter about Holy Angels Nursery wrecked your day then we are now even. You wrecked my night. But beautifully.

Mother's Day ended with a nervous twitch when I learned that your Holy Angels column appeared in the New York Journal American Thursday afternoon—a full weekend ahead of all the other papers, including our own.

It was 10 p.m. when the twitch became unbearable. I tore out to the office, grabbed the key to our Post Office box, opened it and . . .

So you can't hear the angels sing, hey? You're spoofing. I heard them at that moment. They came in clear and strong as I pawed through that river of mail. You want to hear some of the words?

They were Levine and Lastfogel and Lancione. They were Ryan and Dwyer and Chapman and Flynn. They were Jackson and Johnson, MacDonald and Bruns, Tim Murphy and Sophie and a Mary (So help me!) Malone.

That's just a starter, Jim Bishop, of the return addresses on the envelopes.

Home bound like a drunk driver was I with this cargo of mail. Miss Boo and Bill and Debbie and Choo-Choo did some laughing and weeping and barking at that witches hour. Brother-in-law Dave Holmes and nephew David got the news and banged in, wild-eyed, as we ripped into the mail mountain.

We counted dollar bills, Jim Bishop, and fives and tens. We counted checks and money orders, and hours later when it was done and there was little time to sleep, the total was two dollars short of a round number and my flat-topped nephew pulled out his paper-thin wallet and took out the last two pieces of paper.

The total, Jim Bishop? Two thousand ($2,000) dollars.

It was then that everybody else went to bed and the den was quiet, strewn with litter.

It was then that I picked up a letter and felt like a bloody hog.

That's right. A hog. Money. It had come first. Money, then the letters. That was the wrong way—the wrongest of wrong ways.

The letters from all of New York, from Jersey and Pennsylvania and Connecticut were from criminals and judges of criminal courts. They were from children, from poor people, from models and vendors and ad men and news men and copy boys—from housewives and old men. They were from Alice to Zachary, Alpha to Omega and (I swear it) a real John Doe.

Not all of that was from Journal American readers, though. The biggest check of all ($101.50) was from the seventh and eighth grade classes of Elizabeth Lewis and Louise McKittrick in Flint-Groves School, Gastonia. They're our neighbors. Mike Jimison enclosed a poem I'd like you to read some day.

I'm running my mouth too much, Jim Bishop, but it can't keep up with my heart after standing in a red-eyed hour of morning and reading these words from 1812 Bleeker St., Ridgewood, Queens, N.Y.:

"I am very poor at writing letters and not very intelligent. In reading Jim Bishop's column I have come to realize how fortunate my wife and I am.

"We have six children ages two months to 15 years and right now the struggling is tough.

"There is one thing that opened my eyes. Maybe my wife has to wait two years for a new dress or my boys a few weeks longer for a haircut. I still owe the doctor for the last delivery fee. But our children are all healthy.

"It isn't much I have. We have no old or foreign coins but if the good Lord be willing, and I know he will, people will respond because we are all God's children.

"Please accept the little check of $5 enclosed. I wish I were a man like you.

Sincerely,
W. Scheer."

Don't spoof me with more mock toughness. Jim Bishop. Don't tell me you can finish a letter like that except on your knees or with your wet face buried in a rug.

Is there any army you need whipped, Mr. Bishop? Just say so. That's all. One more thing. I'll never be lonely in New York again—not ever. You and your rough, tough,

Yankee friends from Jersey north. Hah! What gorgeous phonies!

Sincerely.
Kays Gary
May, 1973

A Star Is Born

They were all applauding, yelling, stomping or whistling and maybe half of the 9,000 people were out of their seats and on their feet when the big man with the baby face slowly ambled off stage, feeling his way down the steps toward the dressing room.

"Boy!" he breathed, beads of sweat rolling off his cheeks, "Some crowd. What an audience!"

The black man with the smooth, finely-chiseled features, reached out and grabbed a shoulder.

"Well, you really gave it to them," he said. "They're just giving it back. Great show!"

It was an accolade from Charley Pride, the star, The Man, to 31-year-old Ronnie Milsap, blind and awash now with the big, new sound—the roar of the crowd.

Pride meant it. He'd been peeking under the canvas backdrop out onto the stage where spotlights blazed into the upraised glistening face of Milsap, joyously pounding the piano and singing, winging, flying through an encore of a Jerry Lewis medley.

Pride liked what he heard and saw. The crowd was warmed up for the No. 1 man, yet to make his appearance. Later, even as he was similarly baptised by the accustomed accolade, he must have felt it a shade subdued by comparison. When Pride near the end, graciously acknowledged appreciation for the Milsap performance, there was that roar again, decibels above anything he'd heard since coming on stage.

A new star? Ronnie Milsap right up there with Haggard and Pride?

Ronnie stood in the center of fans crowding into the backstage area, smiling, thanking everybody and murmuring about "That crowd . . . It sure turned me on. . . ."

Classmates from his days at the North Carolina State School for the Blind plucked at his sleeve to ask: "Remember me?"

"Lewis Modlin! You wanna wrestle? Dorothy Black . . . Charlie Helms!" Hands touched each other, moved to shoulders and stayed there and there was a whole lot of hugging when the Boyce Atwell family of Pineville came in.

"I reckon you'd call them family," Ronnie said. "I spent happy times with 'em."

"Like my son," Mrs. Atwell said. "He and Larry were roommates. They did so enjoy each other. Larry died nine years ago and Ronnie—Ronnie's here . . . We're so proud."

"When they bought Larry something, they'd buy me something," Ronnie said. "That's like family."

He was glad so many people were proud. It hasn't always been that way.

Born blind in Graham County's mountains, he remembers the arms of a father, of his grandma and grandpa. Loving arms. But some arms were missing and he tried not to think about that. When he reached, though, Grandpa Homer Frisby's hand was there. He was wishing, this night, that Grandpa were here.

"I'd like to have him out there on the stage, that great old feller. He's in his 80's . . . happy up there in Hayesville with his chickens and whittlin'. I sure do wish he could hear this. . . ."

After nine years of playing clubs, rock and pop and country—whatever—Ronnie's star began to rise nine months ago with his first Nashville record: "I Hate You" and "All Together Now, Let's Fall Apart." Top Ten. He landed on "Hee Haw" and the Mike Douglas Show. Credit, he says his manager, Jack Johnson, the man who also put Charley Pride up there.

"I just listen to him, that's all. This isn't a job. This is living. It's fun. I'm trying to get used to big crowds now. Oh, this is great."

There are no tears for Ronnie. Not any you can see anyway. Early on, he decided to enjoy.

He had a scholarship to Emory Law School but there was too much music in him, too much need to play and sing and make the happy scene soaking up people. The focus finally came to country music because "It tells all the stories that everybody feels and hears and understands. And then country music people, the fans, are the most faithful. You can't get 'em down. Mostly I'm singing other people's songs, but maybe someday I can sing the way I feel."

Ronnie Milsap doesn't worry about "getting down" himself, about whether the star will dim or fizzle. He has a wife and a little boy in Memphis and no regrets except . . .

North Carolina, he says, is most generous and "great" in its treatment of handicapped people except he wishes all blind kids could just start in regular school like everybody else. "You're taught that you'll be accepted when you leave

the State school but it doesn't work out that way. Sighted
and blind people are kept apart too long during important
years. It's not their fault but it's a gap that just can't be
closed later. It's a segregation that hangs on hard as
everybody tries."

That said, he called for Steve and introduced him and
said. "He's my main friend. Keeps me straight. Great
drummer, too."

"Can't get away from this fellow," Steve Holt said.
"We've been together five years. I love the man."

With that, Ronnie took the arm of black Steve Holt and,
threading their way through the fans, headed for the exit.

"Don't forget," he called over his shoulder, "I got a
new record coming out. It's called 'Pure Love.' That's a
plug, son!" He was laughing.

February 19, 1974

Elvis Is Comin'

Elvis is a-comin' and the fevers are arisin' and the heart-wrenching appeals to press the flesh or obtain a private moment in The Presence are coming to flood tide.

I wish . . . I DO wish . . . I could help. It would be easier to obtain a private audience with the Pope but Elvis worshipers do not understand this.

I have some difficulty understanding the passion of fans. Failing to understand is not, however, license to ridicule because the passion is real.

There is a lady, for example, wed to the music of a Hawaiian rendition by Elvis only days before her beloved died. She has no ticket. There is no gift which would compare with the opportunity to just hear Elvis sing that song in person, even if she were only standing in some darkened corner, knowing that he knew what singing that song meant.

It's such a little thing and yet a nigh-impossible thing. For the grey-haired little woman it would be something deeply precious for all time.

Heart-wrenching, again, in the manner of the lady's appeal, is a painfully printed "Open Letter To Elvis" from Tammy Ann Miller, age 9, 306-B Hemlock Circle, Lenoir.

"My Daddy got killed in a truck when I was just three years old," Tammy Ann writes. "He looks just like you in lots of his pictures.

"I sing in church. I love to sing 'Amazing Grace' . . . I want to meet you and shake your hand in person when you come to Charlotte. And I would love for you to help me sing two verses of 'Amazing Grace' . . . I want you to autograph a picture so I can remember you. I also know a lady who looks exactly like your mother did . . ."

Well . . .

If I were Col. Tom Parker, Elvis's mentor-manager—Tammy Ann at least would get her wish. And if Elvis knew it she probably would get her wish. There was a time when he drove a truck and did not get killed as did her daddy. There was a time when he sang "Amazing Grace" in church without music. There was a time when he was nine with impossible dreams. Such a meeting would be schmaltzy and public relations cynics would sneer. It's cornball, old-hat and "cheapy" publicity. The Cinderella, sentimental angles are out. The volume of appeals is stupefying.

Besides, neither Elvis nor Col. Parker will read this and the security surrounding his appearance here is tougher than that of Secret Service. It is handled by his own force with its own signals, badges and passwords. The Coliseum people don't know, and don't want to know, where The Man is staying.

We're simply forwarding all this stuff to him at the Coliseum. Col. Parker may or may not pick it up and even if he picks it up . . .

March 5, 1974

There was a girl in Elvis Presley's Coliseum dressing room and Elvis did the only thing a gentleman would do under the circumstances.

He kissed her, touching the silver cross she wore on a necklace.

He did it awkwardly, tenderly and, while he held her, he whispered "Thanks" and the girl's big, brown eyes filled with tears.

Col. Parker looked at little Tammy as Elvis fingered the tiny cross around her neck.

And shifting his cigar, Col. Parker looked down at the tiny purse Tammy Ann carried. In small lettering were the words: "I Love Jesus."

He rapped his cane on the floor, took another look at Tammy Ann and her purse and said: "Well, I took care of you, didn't I?"

Tammy Ann promised to remember the colonel and Elvis the next time she sings "Amazing Grace," probably today, in the Church of God of Resurrection Hope at Whitnel.

March 10, 1974

Buck Young's
Dream Garden:

In a way I wish I hadn't heard of Buck Young.

It messed up a rare moment of self-esteem and satisfaction.

Every man has that feeling when he has just finished putting in a garden with honest sweat, a bone-tired body and high anticipation.

He looks at his neatly rowed and planted patch with a sense of virile satisfaction that his muscles have met and mastered the earth and would, undoubtedly, reap the harvest.

If only nobody had mentioned Buck Young.

The delusion of self-sufficiency is maintained by the new gardener, you see, discounting his investment in lime, fertilizers, soil conditioners, a rented or purchased mechanical tiller, plants and seeds. These things and their costs are taken for granted and properly dismissed lest they dim the rugged self-image.

But it is impossible to dim the image of Buck Young.

Buck Young, from his belt buckle up and from his heart out, is a big man at age 17. The hips, legs and feet hardly merit mention. They don't work. Birth defects are the reason he is less than four feet tall.

Buck Young has other things—a built-in love of people, all people, with a quick smile and flashing, even teeth to show it, plus a burning desire.

The desire: To make things grow and flourish in his care. To make the garden of gardens and then to say, "I did that. Me. Hey, Mamma, help yourself to some beans and pass me another ear of corn!"

He's had that dream a long time and back of the little house at 222 Nodwood, dragging himself on crutches and with a spade in his powerful hands, he has attacked the hard-packed earth in years past without success.

"I'd get a little bit dug up and something planted and then the dogs would run over it or it would die. I just never could make anything grow 'cept in a pot and I want me a real garden," Buck said Saturday.

But this year, days ago, Buck's dream took off as he wistfully watched tractors plow up 12 acres under Duke

Power's transmission lines across from his house.

He scrambled on his crutches to watch them and he had to drop into the damp, newly plowed loam and feel that dirt. Oh, man alive, if he could just get something to plant in that!

Too late, Buck learned that his land, indeed, was being made available free to 20 families of the area. The plots had been allocated by Duke Power because actor Eddie (Green Acres) Albert had done some commercials for Duke. Albert, for payment, had asked the company to do something for low-income families. Duke, with cooperation from Phil Haas and the Agricultural Extension Service, had set up this community vegetable gardening program. The plots were allocated. Duke plowed the land and seeds and fertilizer had been distributed to the families.

Buck hadn't known.

"Our people kept seeing him struggling along on his crutches out there in the plowed ground," Haas said. "You talk with him five minutes and you know something has to be done so we can chisel off a 25 by 50 plot for him. You'd think we gave him the moon."

The seeds and fertilizer were gone but by Saturday Buck had some beans and two packages of corn. He'd put them in the ground, scrambling crab-like between the rows because he has only his arms and hands. He is paralyzed from the waist down.

"I'm goin' to help my mama but I'm goin' to help ME," Buck said Saturday, surveying his land. "Corn, I LOVE. When I get corn it's gonna be butter on one side and teeth on the other and goodby!"

And that isn't all of it, liking corn and "helping Mama," who carries morning and evening paper routes and holds a job in the Law Enforcement Center in between.

"I reckon I want a garden badder'n any these people because . . ."

Buck Young squinted his eyes and his right hand stabbed his crutch into the ground. . . .

"Because I want to see something grow and look at it and say, 'I done that.' I never could do much by myself."

By himself? Haas doesn't see how. Buck can't support his weight on crutches and hoe at the same time. He can't plant and cultivate, just dragging himself along the ground with powerful arms.

Hass remembers a relative, polio-paralyzed, who had a small garden tractor with a hand clutch. He planted and cultivated as he moved it along between the rows.

"If we could find an old garden tractor," Haas said, "I'd rig it up so he'd really have a chance."

"Someday, maybe, I'll get me a ridin' mower to farm up a storm," said Buck, laughing, "but if I can get enough seeds and plants I'm goin' to have me some okra and tomatoes and beans and corn and squashes and cantaloupes and we goin' to eat and eat and eat. And ever'body goin' to know that Buck Young done something himself!"

In a way, I wish I'd never heard of Buck Young. Just when my self-esteem was on the upswing . . .

April 28, 1974

Dirt Farmer

Boredom? Not for Curtis Walker on Carmel Road.

I had decided to drop in on the man who last summer regularly sent checks to Holy Angels Nursery, representing proceeds from sale of garden produce.

The home is a sprawling ranch style on immaculately groomed grounds. Out back I found two Cadillacs, one blue and one gold, in the carport and followed the roar of a motor until I found a lean-jawed angular man in red-clay and sweat-stained denims digging up flower bulbs.

"I'm looking," I said, "for Curtis Walker."

"You found him," he said, wiping his hands on his jeans.

"Getting ready to put in your garden on Good Friday?" I asked.

"Tomorrow's too late," he said. "I've already got it in. Just finished. Now I'm digging up calla lily bulbs, trying to figure what to do with them."

Curtis Walker looks like any of hundreds of dirt farmers I knew in a boyhood spent in upper Cleveland County. The battered hat, the lean, muscle-roped arms, the calloused and work-scarred hands. I told him that's what he looked like.

"That's because I'm off a farm in upper Cleveland County," he said. "Tenant farm 50 years ago. Time or two there we like to starved."

But the house? The Cadillacs? The 26 acres of land in prestigious Carmel?

"I've worked hard, once in chenille manufacturing, then began selling ladies's dresses. Manufacturer's representative. Selling. I did all right, and I bought this land some years ago at the right price."

But now he was showing me the just-planted garden. Neat. Dirt cultivated to fine-grain perfection. Rows as straight as strings on a guitar. Name a vegetable grown in this area, it's in there.

It's a vegetable garden occupying all of a $12,500 lot. He doesn't need the vegetables, and he has more lots, but he does need to make the ground grow things.

"It keeps me alive," he said.

There were times, hard times, when the ground wouldn't yield. And those were the years in upper

Cleveland when "we almost starved."

He was a boy when the Flood of '16 hit, with 42 days and nights of rain, and it was too wet to get into the cotton and when the grass was knee high.

They got the grass out, but the Walkers made only a bale and a half that year, not enough to even pay for the seed and fertilizer when cotton yielded the only cash there was to be had.

"I believe the difference in not starving was trapping rabbits. Rabbit boxes. I caught 28 that winter myself. One rabbit a day for six people. There were four of us kids, and we stayed alive."

Then Curtis Walker was to spend four years in Mills Home, the Baptist Orphanage at Thomasville, and those were years of study and work on the orphanage farm.

He knew about hard farm work and he liked that. Something about doing things for yourself, making things grow, glorying in it in a way maybe only a hungry boy would know.

"I go back up there between Polkville and Casar, and I look at that old place, and it's hard to remember having to live like that. But then, even with the sight of those mountains just a way off, you do remember.

"And I remember the year after the flood when my daddy's cottonseed wasn't coming up, and somebody told him it looked like it wouldn't. I remember he said, 'It'll come up because it HAS to come up. Tom Stamey at the store has a mortgage on everything.' "

Curtis Walker took me to a shed and showed me an expensive small tractor and then another tractor he likes best because it has handles like plow handles and you hold and handle them the way you would with a mule-drawn plow.

And he proudly showed off his discs and an old middle-buster, the turning plow and the cotton cultivator plow to bite down deep for sub-soiling. And over yonder across the road were stables where he gets his manure. No chemical fertilizers.

"I could have retired, maybe should have retired, but the company keeps wanting me to stay a little longer. I've cut down to three days a week now so I can work in dirt."

With his orphanage background and surplus vegetables he decided to let people come and buy last summer and send the money each week to Holy Angels. He intends to do the same this summer.

As for those thousands of calla lily bulbs, double-blooming, blood-red President variety, he was trying to figure what to do with them. That decision came quickly enough.

Next week, from Wednesday on, he'll sell them at $12 per 100 to anyone who comes by, again with all proceeds to the Nursery.

As for the Cadillacs in the carport . . .

"That's where I like to see them. Great when you're on the road, but I'm really living when I'm handling a tractor."

Sweating in the dirt of a $12,500 garden plot.

That, for Curtis Walker, is the ultimate in luxury.

April 20, 1973

Wedding Chimes

Her voice sounded both old and young. There were cracks in it. There was vibrant warmth in it.

The address she gave is on Charlotte's Mink Lane.

And her request was, she feared, a little strange.

"You won't think I'm foolish?"

"No, ma'am."

"It's about this little girl . . . a naive, sweet little thing she is . . . who does my nails at the beauty parlor. She's getting married Sunday."

"Yes, ma'am."

"She likes the chimes she hears from somewhere out there. There won't be any chimes at her wedding in South Carolina.

"Well, I . . ."

"Wait a minute. One evening not long ago the chimes were playing 'Bells Of St. Mary's' when she was leaving work. 'I wish,' she's said two or three times since, 'I could hear Bells of St. Mary's when I leave for the last time Friday.'

"Will you find the bells for her? Would you have them play that? I know it sounds crazy sentimental but I've been married 32 years and she's so young and it would be something she'd always remember."

There wasn't much time.

Religion Editor Roy Covinging helped. We screened the churches that might have chimes in that area. It was not the First Christian Church . . . not Dilworth Methodist nor Myers Park Methodist. It was not Covenant, St. Luke's Lutheran, St. Patrick's Catholic, Myers Park Presbyterian, nor Ascension Lutheran nor the Little Church On The Lane.

But the chimes were found. And the chimes played "Bells Of St. Mary's" on Friday. They rang out at noon and they rang out at 6 o'clock when the little manicurist put away her kit and walked out of the shop and stopped and stood alone.

Once Joan D'Arc may have worn the same look when she heard The Voices. Her smile was that of an angel.

There was a smile, too, on a face reflecting on 32 years of marriage in a big and elegant home.

We did not see the face belonging to the hands that set

the chimes to playing.

But we know, at this moment, it was the most beautiful and certainly the most courageous face of the three.

For she sat alone and played the chimes at the place she is staying for a time—in the chapel of the Florence Crittenton Home for unwed mothers.

July 13, 1958

The Littl'uns

Papa Keith Webber of Boone was puzzled as he observed daugher Amy, 2½, peer down the front of her dress, turning her head this way and that and frowning as she tugged. "Just what," he asked, "are you doing?"

Still intent in her efforts Amy didn't bother to look up. "I'm listenin'," said she. "My stomach is talkin' and I can't tell what it's saying!"

May 22, 1974

Political and Social Commentary

Everybody knows that Kays Gary has the ability to touch people deeply with his columns, particularly with stories about the heroic, the tragic, the young or the old. He writes about people in ways that sharpen our appreciation of the mystery and wonder of life.

But many of us forget that Kays can also be a social and political critic with the power to challenge old attitudes, stir new thought. I remember a column he wrote that attacked the John Birch Society for arousing suspicions that had in the past proved more menacing to society than any imagined threat that communists were hiding under official beds. I remember another about his distaste for people who at Christmas or Thanksgiving thought it was "time to do good to others" and called up charitable agencies in search of a family "deserving" of their beneficence. Another pointed up the folly of people who, forgetting the help they received along the way, call on others to lift themselves by their own bootstraps.

Kays knows politics and politicians well. In his early days on The Observer, his column was entitled "People and Politics." When the occasion demands, he can still turn a telling phrase to puncture a pompous office holder or revive a hidden social or political truth. Some examples are in this collection.

Jack Claiborne

Dorothy Counts

A head needs no face for expression.
The way it is carried upon the neck tells all.
If it is too high it shows defiance.
If it is low and twists from side to side with a for-
ward thrust of the neck it is full of shame.

Between these extremes is the posture of dignity and
confidence, and a certain blend of humility and pride.

And that is the way she carried her head.
They spat and she was covered with it.
Spittle dripped from the hem of her dress.
It clung to her neck and her arms and she wore it.
They spat and they jeered and screamed.

A boy tumbled out of the crowd and hit her in the
back with his fist.

Debris fell on her shoulders and around her feet.
And the posture of the head was unchanged.
That was the remarkable thing.
And if her skin was brown you had to admit that her
courage was royal purple.
For how many of us could have taken that walk to
and from a school?

September 5, 1957

(Dorothy Counts was the first black to attend a Charlotte
all-white public school, three years after the landmark
desegregation decision of Brown vs. Board of Education.
Her story appeared nationwide.)

Psychology of a Race Riot

What is really the backbone of "demonstrations?" The single incidents that flare into race riots?

The black man who stopped by my desk had his own ideas.

"The main thing isn't just the obvious issue, some segregated place that is being picketed, or some isolated incident; it is the endless experience of countless indignities.

"People may wonder why so much fuss over a bowling alley or a laundry. It isn't just the bowling alley or a laundry. It is having authoritative illiterates constantly calling you 'Boy' when you're a man with a Master's degree.

"It is being talked to in public like an animal instead of a human being. It is being called "Daisy" during an interview when your name is plainly "Mrs. Daisy Jones" on the application. It is being mocked in your own dialect by somebody who doesn't have that dialect. It is being told to wait in some place apart from the place whites may be waiting.

"It is being a Negro serviceman back from Vietnam and visiting a doctor's office where he is ordered to sit in the colored waiting room. He is back from a place where the foxholes were not segregated and where the white and black bodies were lined up side by side. Do you meekly follow the orders? Would you?

"Now a doctor, say, or a nurse could say this is private property and it is their right to have anybody sit where they're told but do they accept responsibility for the reaction? Huh-uh. But they're right in there, baby, in the mind if not on a picket sign.

"Well, people who do these things are responsible. You don't demonstrate because somebody calls you "boy" or because of any of these little things. But this is what is going on out there when the streets are angry and the fellow who did it isn't just that guy who wants to keep Negroes out of his bowling alley. It is all those people who get their kicks out of psychologically kicking a 'nigger'."

February 24, 1968

Martin Luther King

What is left to say, now?

The grief and guilt pour out and into one great vessel of man's confession of his inadequacy. They are poured and they boil and steep then in agonies.

There are screams and shouts and curses and prayers and mutilations of our souls and passions in another midnight of our life and times.

But there is more.

The vilification that came to Martin Luther King, as it comes to all spiritual revolutionists, suddenly stuck in the throats that once so open were now constricted.

There came, perhaps slowly, a realization among multitudes—dim and inadequate as it might be—of who and what he was and who is left and what is left to take his place.

Because of this, it can be desperately hoped that Martin Luther King in death will serve mankind even greater than he did in life. This is the history of the great martyrs. The terrible truth in death will not be denied nor is there any hiding from it.

Thousands and tens of thousands and millions now will read his words in depth and will come to know the man and his mission as never before.

Those among us, and they were legion, who knew Martin Luther King only as a Negro leader in the midst of multitudes and strife and thus ascribed to him all manner of self-serving, destructive and demagogic intents, now are forced to face the blinding martyr's light.

I was most struck by the flood of calls, particularly from mothers and the young, which followed the assassination. They were not calls of fear but instead were calls of deep sadness. "What can we DO?" was the question most often asked. "I am so busy with the children, the PTA, the church, committee meetings. Maybe I attended the wrong meetings. Maybe I, like so many others, failed to speak our minds when we should have spoken."

That is the way it went and from the tone it would seem that these were not merely and temporary spasms of a cataclysmic hour.

As for the violence, the complete antithesis and—in truth—revilement of the central purpose of Martin Luther

King's life, it must be stopped. But just as importantly it must be understood. And it can be understood if we place ourselves in some common time and circumstance of cruelly assaulted innocence and feel again the mindless savagery that seemed to burst our vessels and our brain.

Martin Luther King is dead but in death he breathed life into the central truth of our creation so powerfully that neither white nor black shall ever be able to conquer it with guns or knives, bombs or flames.

Sadly, tragically, men will try to do this.

Joyfully, certainly, they will fail.

April 7, 1968

Aren't Winners
Always Right?

Kate Smith, said the fellow on the phone, is just the one to put this country back on its feet.

"Kate Smith?" I said.

"That's right," he said. "I've called CBS and I've called WBT and there are just five hours left. Now I know you can do it if anybody can—get Kate Smith on that program tonight when the peace is signed."

Well, on rainy Saturday afternoons one has time to listen, even to a voice bearing a trace of having quaffed oft and deeply.

"Sure. Remember how she used to sing 'God Bless America'? You get her on there and end that program with her singing 'God Bless America' and . . . Remember the Big War? You remember how it was when she sang 'God Bless America'? I want you to know I've got my flag flying out front and if this whole country could just hear her sing it the way she used to it would be like old times. The country would get that old feelin'."

To some, the hacked old veteran's hopes-and-sentiment inspired ideas might have seemed comical or ridiculous but to us it was forlorn.

We wish we could just blame it all on a rainy Saturday and pretend that this is just one odd-ball whose feeling will pass.

And yet, he isn't alone in longing for a return to what he thought was a better day, when people thought they were sure about what they believed. We're a people who have always been winners and, after all, aren't winners always right?

But we've had other calls, other letters, reflecting a longing for something to believe in and reflecting despair because it isn't easy any more.

Take one from a college professor remarking on our recent columns about Charlotte's Caroline Elliott, volunteer with a Quaker team working among the war-shattered bodies of Vietnam and herself disturbed about what kind of country we are:

"These columns moved me," the professor wrote, "as nothing in fiction about war or current news accounts about war has moved me.

"Leaving the hell-hole of South Vietnam, one can't go back to childhood innocence and unquestioning faith in the forces of good over evil. One can't go back to the childhood response to 'The Star-Spangled Banner'." One can't go back to the sad-but-unlived attitude about loving one's neighbor as one's self. One can't go back to the pseudo-intellectual atmosphere of the college classroom where issues are discussed objectively and analytically, far removed from the actual circumstances. . . .

"So many can never go home again."

When the news of the war's end occurred, the news media were prepared and straining—ready to report the reaction. It was eerie. There was no emotional outpouring of relief or anything else, which is not to say that no one felt anythng. The feeling, we suspect, was unexpressed because there are no words for emptiness.

And not even Kate Smith could bring back that old feeling.

We had achieved, we were told, "peace with honor" and if this were true, why didn't we feel it?

We searched and are searching for some sign beyond business-as-usual.

The stock market dropped. Some months ago the market rallied, analysts told us, because of "increased optimism" about prospects for peace. Conversely, any reverses were explained by snags in the peace talks. Now it's over and why does the market slide? Is it because Kate Smith hasn't sung "God Bless America"?

There was a time. Our spirits soared when John Kennedy said: "Ask not what your country can do for you; ask what you can do for your country." Why, then, didn't we feel it when President Nixon paraphrased the Kennedy challenge to have us ask not what the government could do for us but what we can do for ourselves?

Most of us, I suspect, are and have been right busy doing for ourselves without a lot of satisfaction. Whatever satisfaction we get is from the fact or illusion of doing for others.

And this time, in Vietnam, we didn't save the world again.

Perhaps in time this sense of emptiness will pass.

Perhaps, now with war's end, the deeply held religious convictions Billy Graham is convinced belong to President Nixon, can manifest themselves in forging a new and responsible, prideful and caring role for America.

We've got to have it. Self-sufficiency is only a part of our heritage. The greater part of it, the spiritually ennobling part, is caring about the real dignity of all our brothers—the tired, the poor, the oppressed and exploited.

As for God blessing America . . .

He has already done that.

On the other hand . . .

January 28, 1973

The Cherubs Aren't Singing

The honeymoon is over.

There was sweet pathos about it while it lasted. Bruised and hungry hearts picked up a stronger beat. The long, dry thirst for nourishment in the faith of our fathers seemed about to end.

And now.

The honeymoon is over and the faith of our fathers has turned to Monday dust.

This commentary is not my professional duty. Mine is to let the sunshine in, to play the flute so that cherubs sing at heathen fests. But this commentary I claim as a right after 28 years as a newsman, almost 54 years as a citizen imbued from childhood with the idea that my country is the last best hope for consummating the second sentence of the Lord's Prayer.

And now.

President Ford has granted, in advance, a full pardon to former President Nixon for any and all federal crimes he may have committed.

I am outraged and no riptide of "What about Chappaquidick?" will change that.

The man just pardoned faced evidence, rather than speculation, that cold sober he directed crimes against the Constitution, assaults against principles established as the bedrock of this country and compounded deceit against the people who gave him the most precious gift in their power. He is pardoned.

Who can declare, ever again, that in America every man stands equal before the law?

Who can, ever again, be shocked at the breakdown of law and order when its chief apostle has profaned its trust?

Who can, ever again, demand that punishment be swift and sure in the name of Justice?

What do we tell the Boy Scouts? The bright young faces in classrooms? Our youth errant in their defiance of our claimed morality?

What do we say to those guilty of crimes of momentary passion? To the deprived, sub-intellects who assault and rob, taking what they cannot earn? What do we say to those whom we have caged, segregated from contact with our pious persons?

Shall we say that the right to lie, to cheat, to steal belongs only to those whose mastery of deceit can first carry them to highest places?

What shall we say to deserters whose only crime was fear? Or to thousands of young whose conscience told them "Thou shalt not kill" is a law stronger than that of Selective Service?

Recall it, now.

We cheered or added prayerful "Amens" when our President said that to grant amnesty to these would bring dishonor to those who fought so gallantly, some dying, in Vietnam.

Now a president, pardoned in advance for high crimes and misdemeanors, voices no such anguish for dishonor brought thus to the tombs of Washington, of Jefferson, of Lincoln.

He is in anguish, we are told. The act of mercy was extended to relieve it.

Yet that anguish has never penetrated the heart of a man to the extent of publicly acknowledging other than "mistakes."

Richard Nixon has never and will never ask the American people's forgiveness, and it is to be strongly suspected that in that twisted person writhes the suspicion that he does not need to. That in this, the ninth or 10th or 20th-whatever crisis of Richard Nixon, the seed of his justification may still be alive in the hearts of many.

If this be true it is time for the funeral of the great American experiment. It is time, indeed, for the benediction.

Certainly there are ambivalent feelings in the most partisan hearts about what the law should have done to Richard Nixon.

It is to no man's credit to wish for him a sentence in jail as received by other mere mortals for lesser crimes.

Yet the pardoning seems to have done more than save him from jail. Instead, it places truth behind bars, buries it in a dungeon, stifles it to the point that rumor and distortion may yet bring a someday resurrection of the politics of pious infidels. That is the risk of it and the tragedy of it.

Though it is a documented matter of history more than 30 years after the fact there are those in Germany who consider the genocide of World War II a fairy tale. It is one way of burying guilt and keeping alive the promise that Hitler's Germany may rise again.

And now.

President Ford, most would likely agree, acted in good conscience. Richard Nixon was a close friend. For more than 60 per cent of us, he was more than a friend. He was, if you please, a "return to honor and decency," to "old-fashioned values." For that reason many find condemnation of Richard Nixon a condemnation of self and cannot, just as he cannot, bring themselves to do it.

But I must and for the record.

No matter what the Dow-Jones does today I can hear no cherubs sing.

September 10, 1974

No Tears for Dobie

Heave no sad sighs for Dobie.

And let no heart bleed for his Ma.

Few there are with such happiness.

Dobie is a good boy. Age 38.

He is a man in many ways—in responsibility, in physical strength.

But a raging fever as a child made him a child forever in the things that matter most.

Dobie's trust of all is infinite.

His God is 'way up high in the sky and listening.

And his Mama is in the kitchen.

If she is in the kitchen she is cooking and she is singing.

But though she is old she has good reasons.

Or if she is sick abed no one need fear.

Dobie, strong and smiling, is there.

Tenderly he places cooling cloth on head and fetches the medicines. Eagerly he prepares her tray with soup and spoon . . .

. . . And a tiny blossom from some secret place. No matter what the season there are flowers somewhere for Dobie.

And in the good, strong outside sun his muscled arms swing true the ax to split the wood for hearth and stove.

Dobie likes to work . . . to swing the ax and dig the earth and hear his Mom croon, "So proud . . . oh, Dobie you're the best."

She means it. Six sons she had. All are good men.

Important men, too. They have their families and they've made their marks . . . in cities scattered around the compass and afar.

All but Dobie.

Dobie saved her from a back bedroom in some suburban place, or apartment in the city, or yet, perhaps, a nursing home.

And she can watch him sitting there in the big chair, the firelight tossing shadows across the handsome manchild's face, and scarcely keep from shouting it for all to hear.

But they all know and marvel in that place. There is no man to tease their Dobie. And if one should he'd best make tracks to keep his health.

For Dobie is friend and guardian of all good, living, growing things. And better than most he knows the rights from wrongs.

It has been long years since a threat to this serenity occurred. It came with the war.

Dobie didn't want to leave his Ma but he knew he was a man with many debts to pay.

And so he made his way to enlist.

And they told him: "Dobie, we need you. Everybody needs you. But we need you on the farm worst of all. Please stay and grow things for us . . ."

But not a month passed but that Dobie went back to enlist . . . to see if things were so bad they'd need him in the Army instead of the farm . . . but each time they begged him to keep working at home.

Finally the war was over.

And other boys came home with ribbons and citations and things. They were not alone.

And none were half so proud as Dobie with the official and framed citation signed by the entire draft board:

"In recognition and highest appreciation of Dobie ————'s valor, loyalty and untiring efforts contributing to victory for freedom's cause . . . "

Dobie's finest hours are not done. His church just finished its new and beautiful sanctuary. The congregation elected many new officers. Not the least of these was Dobie.

With the knowledge that he would never fail them, they unanimously elected him to one of the most responsible positions of all.

Dobie will be the ringer of the bell.

In places there may be women weeping for small sons marked "Retarded."

But if they listen carefully, in the way of Dobie's Ma, they may yet hear the angels sing . . . to the ringing of a bell.

September 15, 1959

One Wet Whisper

Type-casting can be both blessing and curse.

Actors, writers, committee chairmen, chefs—all resist it.

A juvenile star has trouble getting out of short pants before he is 40. A ticket chairman who goes over the top never gets a chance to perform. He's ticket chairman forever.

Concoct a new and different salad and your world becomes a bowl of endives and old lettuce.

Dip a pen in pathos and you write a one-way ticket to waterfalls of tears.

"Oh," says the lady to whom you've just been introduced, "you're the man whose job is to tug at the heart strings!"

It is like a lash of the whip.

The juvenile actor would play Don Juan . . . the ticket chairman would sing "Aida" . . . salad-maker dreams of pork chops . . . the sob-sister would cut at hard, cold facts.

A classroom of retarded children is hardly the place to begin cutting cold, hard facts. But resolve is high.

How much money does the state spend for this? How much is given by agencies and individuals? And why, since such children can never learn from books?

You are going to the Lakeview School classroom of Mrs. Nancy Byrum and her assistant, Miss Narvie Johnson. The children are ages six to 12. Their mental ages are two and three. They are not educable. They are trainable. Some have limited power of speech. Some have none.

What does this mean? It means they can learn to do some things . . . by habit . . . by rote . . . by association. They can be taught to give a certain response to a familiar situation. They can develop personalities.

It is hard to concentrate on these objective things with a little mongoloid hugging your neck because you looked at the jig-saw puzzle he was trying to do and patted him on the head.

It is hard to be coldly objective when Mrs. Byrum calls each, one by one, to another table and they promptly, smilingly obey.

You watch them sit, hands in lap as they have been taught, until each has been given crayons and paper with different shapes to color.

"Find the green crayon, now, and color the circle green," Mrs. Byrum says.

Some pick out brown crayons, some yellow, some green. But soon all except one little girl have found the green crayon. She picks up first one and then the other. She looks, hopefully, at Mrs. Byrum. You look out the window and wait, realizing your teeth are beginning to clench. Finally there is applause.

The last little girl has found the right crayon.

Then a handsome, brown-eyed little fellow who keeps wanting to sit by you goes up and whispers to Mrs. Byrum. She nods. Proudly, he leaves the room. He is going to the bathroom. By himself.

When the coloring is over the children put the crayons away—in the right box.

They have already had the morning opening of the pledge to the flag and the singing of the national anthem. But they want to do it again. For you.

They do this. You understand some of the words. Mostly you understand the look in their eyes. Solemnly, this thing is done. One boy shocked even Mrs. Byrum by saying the pledge all by himself.

Then here is your new, brown-eyed buddy, back again, to make like a boxing match. It is a game he invented. Pretend to box him. He falls over in a mock faint. Then all the children count: "One . . . two . . . three . . . four . . . five . . . six . . ."

This way, they learn.

They learn from pictures, too.

Mrs. Byrum holds up a picture of a child praying.

"Pway . . . Pway . . . Guhl is pwaying!"

And they fold their hands and get down on their knees. Quietly, they pray their different prayers.

Brown Eyes, your buddy, is saying, "Now I lay me . . ."

You try to think of clinical things . . . like costs and teacher training and . . .

Now Mrs. Byrum holds up a picture of a boy whispering to a girl.

"Can you do what he is doing?" she says.

They can. They begin whispering to each other. All except Brown Eyes. He climbs on your lap and grabs your head fiercely between his hands and whispers wetly in your ear.

You have to go. In a hurry. No time to explain. The
story must wait until another time. You are type-cast. You
are a prisoner.

Brown Eyes ruined cold resolve with that wet whisper.
He said: "I wuv you, Daddy!"

                                        November 11, 1959

An Old Fisherman's Memories

Sitting there on the river bank he looked like anything but a fisherman enjoying his golden years.

The fish weren't biting. But that wasn't all.

"Can't git me no job," he said. "Got a no-good heart. Got a no-good back. Ain't done me no wuk in five years . . ."

He had, for sure, the miseries. Non-alcoholic but 100 proof.

But memories?

A grin split his round, black face.

"Oh, yeh!" he said. "You lookin' at the best cook what ever come down the road!"

Time was, he said, when he took his chef's hat off to no man. Never learned readin' and never learned writin' but his mammy had taught him cookin' down in the East Carolina swamp country. He'd gone on to cooking game and barbecue at the hunting lodges and seafood on the coast and he'd got to be so great a lady with a Florida hotel practically kidnaped him to work for her. And he had—eight years. Eight big years.

"Man, I cook the pheasant and the big old snappers. I cook the sweetbreads . . . Lawd, I cook it all . . . An' big rich folks come back to the kitchen makin' over me and wantin' recipes. Haw! They don't believe I ain't got none of it wrote down 'cept in my head. Lawd, them folks love me!"

Then his heart had gone bad and he'd come home to the swamp country to get well, only he hadn't, and the day came he had to get a piece of work and he took a day job rolling a wheelbarrow full of bricks. He fell off a trestle.

"Bus' my back," he said. "Can't stand up no time."

One thing keeps him going, he said.

"If it wasn't for that reckon I might just slide on down in the river with them fish. I got it here."

From an otherwise empty wallet he drew out a yellowed piece of stationery, sweat-stained and almost disintegrated at the folds.

"That there tells you what kinda man I am," he said, and his eyes began to mist. "It's from the hotel lady where

I wuk. She beg me to come back. She say how they missed me and how couldn't never nobody cook like me. It's down there in writin'."

He unfolded the paper carefully and handed it over.

He'd 'bout memorized it, he said, because he could not read. Doctor had read it to him when it had arrived years ago. The doctor had read it to him a bunch of times, he said.

"Read it out loud," he said.

A swift glance and we begged off. Left our spectacles somewhere.

A quivering forefinger pointed over our shoulder and to the signature.

"That's her," he said. "That's my boss lady. She sure pour it on, don't she?"

We reckoned. And then some, as we read a resort hotel's mimeographed form letter 14-Y. His name had been filled in at the top.

"Our summer rates with a 10 per cent discount take effect May 1," it said. "Our summer patrons will be the first to enjoy the latest and finest in luxury living, result of a just completed modernization program which includes . . ."

Gentle fingers took the letter . . . reverently folded and tucked it back into the wallet.

"I tole you!" he said, smiling. "Like the lady said, one time I was the best cook that ever come down the road!"

April 26, 1962

The Time Is
Almost Here

The time is almost here.

With friends and relatives taken care of in wild sprees of imprudent spending will come the annual awakening of conscience.

The search for "a poor family" will begin.

Some of us would first determine . . . er-ah . . . "Are they white or colored? Not that it makes any difference . . ."

And the family should be "worthy." The "worthy" condition has varying interpretations but a concensus would suggest that those worthy of our personal benevolence would be:

1. Too proud to be on "welfare."

2. Eager candidates for church but for lack of shoes.

3. Abstainers from tobacco, alcohol, profanity and other evidences of immorality.

4. Able to show a proper but not embarrassing measure of appreciation, preferably in silent tears.

The exaggeration is slight. Our visions are of the poor-but-pure, the little match girl, Tiny Tim, St. Peter in masquerade, Mary Magdalene washed in the blood.

The celebrated birthday is that of total selflessness, total humility, total mercy and total forgiveness.

What mockery . . . what pomposity . . . what pathetic caricature it is that man presents with his conditional beneficence!

In silent, trembling moments the soul writhes if it dares confront its inconsistency. It shrivels in contemplation of a someday accounting as harsh as the judgments it has held for others.

What irony there is in our twin disciplines.

The one allows frivolous purchase of some expensive and nonsensical bauble for personal laughs.

The other is rooted in deepest concern that the ultimate recipient of a Christmas basket be worthy of the gift.

None of us should escape concern lest Christmas become not merely an orgy of self-indulgence but something little better—a time for ridding ourselves of guilt in one shot at bargain basement prices.

The Star heralded love and love isn't cheap and it isn't easy and it is giving and caring without a signed receipt.

The people who need are out there.

Many of them drink. Most of them smoke. Most are profane.

There are 12-year-old boys responsible for five younger brothers and sisters, shoeless, cold, hungry . . . 12-year-old boys with the responsibility of men and total strangers to a kind word, a single sign that anyone cares.

There are girls like this and toddlers who would spit in your eye or conk you with a rock for no reason.

The poor and loveless are out there. It takes little effort to find them.

All of them have broken some commandments. Some of them have broken all commandments. Some of them don't even know what the commandments are.

That is the way it was 2,000 years ago.

That is why Christmas began.

That is what Christmas is—hope for the hopeless, love for the unlovely and unloved.

The time is almost here . . .

December 8, 1965

Kid Cruelty Scars Forever

Confession.

Every time I witness cruelty of children toward children there is a mixture of anger and guilt searing to the bone.

The anger is knowing there is no wound as deeply felt as that inflicted by one's peers. There is no torment like rejection.

The guilt is remembering that as a 13-year-old I regularly mimicked a fellow, who, because of a childhood bout with encephalitis, talked and walked abnormally. Others laughed. So did he for that matter and in turn mimicked me and MY bow-legged walk, laughing like thunder and giving as good as he got.

The thing was, there was nothing wrong with Jeff's brain. He was an extraordinary fellow. Everybody liked having him around. Nobody ran from him and if anyone had laid a hand on Jeff, he would have paid dearly.

Still I will be forever plagued with guilt for having made fun of him even without cruel intent. It was savagery, still, and why didn't I know?

In this business, I am regularly reminded of the maiming force of cruelty. I see it with youngsters forever called "Fatso" or "Bug-Eye" or "Runt" or any one of scores of scornful epithets some of us of other generations seemed to survive. But then, no one has kept count of how many of us were permanently scarred by rejection in the form of habitual cruelty.

I thought of it days ago in the case of the Union County child who, accidentally or otherwise, burned himself to death. There was some evidence he had been unable to suffer taunts and teasing at school—to the point that he dreaded it as true torture. Whatever other problems the little boy had, this certainly was a factor in the tragedy.

Since that terrible event I have heard from mothers of other children similarly plagued. One, whose child is brain-damaged and crippled, had even suffered assaults in the neighborhood and been the victim of injurious hoaxes. A counselor advised he be given a course in karate to build his confidence and ability to defend himself.

Karate was a crashing failure as he sobbingly declared, "I don't want to hurt or be hurt."

For this the kid is a coward? Scratch it. Some of us would be lovers, not fighters.

Young people have come a long way since my day in compassion and empathy toward less fortunate peers. I see this especially among high schoolers who push wheelchairs for friends, assist others with problems in sight or hearing. Yet, at elementary and junior high levels, at the most vulnerable age there are those who, as did I, play to the crowd at the expense of somebody who is "different." It is psychological assault inflicting wounds as permanently as any knife.

To my dying breath I'll never forget Jeff.

And there is nothing that could make me prouder than to have a child of mine befriend and defend a handicapped peer.

1974

Kids, We're All Handicapped

Judging from the phone calls there are kids a-plenty who suffer the slings and arrows of epithets and harassment by their peers. It was ever so, a part of childhood most of us are glad to forget.

A few, to their detriment, never do, allowing the cruelties of others to color their lives with timidity at best, bitterness and despair at worst.

Tuesday's column was a comment on the cruelty of children toward children who are "different" in looks, manner, speech or achievement. It was prompted by speculation on the torment of a Union County youngster who recently burned himself to death, accidentally or otherwise, because of his treatment by others.

So the phone began ringing early Tuesday. Parents a-plenty are confronted with the problem. Most of them were grateful that the problem was publicly acknowledged. They, as well as their children, had the feeling they were singular in coping with it—alone.

Parental awareness is important. To sympathize is not enough. To tell the child to "pay no attention" to his tormentors is a cheap cop-out. It won't make them or the problem go away.

The best a parent can do is to be honestly concerned and find a way to help the child build and reinforce self-esteem.

"To read a comment in defense of the 'different' was a help in itself," one father said. "My son and I read it together at breakfast this morning. He has a speech problem. He stutters. He has been terrified to read aloud at school. This morning he decided the next time anybody laughs he will laugh with them."

Perhaps he will even learn to tell his peers, "Look, my problem is obvious. What is yours and can I help?"

And the child who gets his kicks at someone else's expense DOES have a problem. If a kid feels compelled to damage someone's ego his own has to be in pretty bad shape. In the long haul he's the guy who may have the biggest problem since he isn't even aware of it. To late he may discover a mature society turns its back on an insensitive bully.

Whatever the problem, any parent can find parallels among successful men and women in history and now. Short people, tall people, crippled people, people who flunked geography, people who stutter, people with bad eyes, lantern jaws, receding chins, whatever. What kind of a world would it be if all the guys looked like Robert Redford and the other half like Farrah Hyphen? And imagine a perfect society peopled by nothing but Howard Cosells!

Wonder where all the kids are who figured Mel Tillis would never get past the gas pumps with that stuttering problem? And how come one-eyed Sandy Duncan keeps popping up in TV films and commercials? With that face how did Phyllis Diller escape a career stopping clocks? And with those legs why didn't Franklin Roosevelt just stick with his stamp collection? With those ears what made Clark Gable think he could become an idol of women the world over? And whatever made that runt Paul Williams think he could write music and be in demand on practically every TV show on the charts?

Hey, kids, we're ALL handicapped. But we were all created with the seed of something like glory to tip the scales even-up and better in the sum of things and we'd better believe it.

But it's tough to be Pollyanna when you're down. Just believe some of us remember how painful it was. I didn't like the nickname "Runt" and I liked the next one, "Drip," even less. But, looking back, I wouldn't trade places with the dudes who pinned them on me.

And David Lawrence, who at age 34 became editor of The Observer, won't even reveal what his nickname was. He isn't about to go through THAT again!

Self-pity and martyrdom won't put a stop to the persecution.

Nor will a counterpunch, though it's sometimes inevitable and good for the soul.

Persistent dignity and thoughtfulness are weapons the tormentors can't handle. They stop 'em cold.

February 8, 1977

Who Can Say
'Let Them Die'?

When do you let them go?

The right-to-die issue is turned inside out by social and professional forces. Magazines and journals are full of it. It will never be fully or exactly resolved because there comes a moment when no man can easily say, "Now."

Some physicians are beginning to share a burden they've borne alone. Some will speak, guardedly, about a point when the question is, "Am I prolonging life or am I really prolonging death?'

And others have to help him answer that question.

Once in my life I have had to make that decision. Once more it has been thrust at me.

I speak to the pitiful, withered shape of my once-beautiful mother and she cannot reply. For hours on end the head droops, facial features contoured in silent agony. The heavy rattle in her throat and chest bring weak and constant coughs. Great purple blotches spread slowly over skin hanging loosely from her frame. When the eyes open they stare aimlessly, unfocused, at nothing.

One talks of the years ago, of children, of her mother and sisters and of good times and loving times in an aimless monologue, hoping for a reaction. For something. Even an easy sigh instead of the small snore, the hurtful twitches and spasms, the deep rattle in the chest.

Until this, for years her days had been those of a child, reaching for a caress, smiling at a tender touch, with fleeting moments of reincarnation as the always gentle, gracious and compassionate lady and hostess.

But even that was gone, gone forever, and sitting there stroking the furrowed brow one would know she would never have accepted this. Even she, who never protested in behalf of self all her life, could not accept this humiliation, this death beyond death. How can we of health and reason selfishly cling?

These thoughts, all these, were tumbling, racing through a surrendered grief. For days she had not responded and there still she lay, all crumpled until . . .

Suddenly, quite suddenly, the eyes opened and for fleeting seconds they shone even as her brows arched in the old familiar way.

"Well!" she exclaimed and just as suddenly she was gone again. Again she had become the withered, moaning stranger.

But there had been that moment of the blue-eyed smile, so fleeting it seemed a thing imagined. Except it wasn't.

A single fleeting moment and the right-to-die debate was finished for now. A single fleeting smile and eyes alight with life put out all the fires.

November 18, 1977

[Lettie M. Gary, Kays's mother, died March 10, 1978.]

Woman's Story
Of Hurt, Shame

Her obsession is less than magnificent, and it won't let
her go.

That is why I found myself—again—cast presump-
tuously in the role of a priest in a booth of a midtown coffee
shop.

When first I looked directly into her eyes I wished I
hadn't come. There was too much hurt there; hurt and
something more.

She had the look of a lady, thirtyish, smartly dressed,
softly feminine but not overtly sexy. There was an occa-
sional tremor at the corners of her mouth, and as she tried
to get out the words her eyes would fill, but not quite spill,
the tears.

"This man," she began, "was the first and the only
one, if you can believe it. It was so wrong. He was, is, married; but he was so fine, so sensitive. No man in any city
would have a better reputation with more people."

I could have guessed the rest. My mind raced ahead.
What was I doing here? This would be a dead end. I wanted
to stop it right there. The eyes wouldn't let me.

"You see, I've always been a faithful church person
and this gentleman, this man, is widely known and
respected, a leader in his church and community. He is a
celebrity, a moral celebrity, and he is wealthy. I suppose I
thought he was as good as God. He couldn't do anything
wrong. Maybe I told myself that to convince myself it
wasn't wrong."

"I believe," I said, "you need professional counseling,
not me."

"I wanted that," she said. "He's against it. He won't
pay for it, either. He wouldn't pay for anything. But it isn't
the money. Honestly. Let me tell you, let me ask you . . .

"When I learned I was pregnant I met him. I told him.
He said 'abortion.' He said he'd be ruined, his whole career.
His wife would take everything. I had to have an abortion.
I didn't want that. I don't believe in it. But I have my
career, too. Finally, I begged. I had to have his support in
whatever happened. 'Yes,' he said, 'yes.' "

Her eyes filled again. "Only a woman can know . . . I

never knew and I can't explain the horror of that experience. Alone. He wasn't there. He didn't call. Later, days later, he wanted to see me again and he gave me an envelope. Do you know what was in it? Fifty dollars. Five tens. I felt like the lowest . . . I couldn't believe he . . .

"He wanted us to go on and to his favorite place—a cemetery. That's when this thing took hold of me that I can't be rid of. He goes on, worshiped by everyone every day. I'm left in ruins, like dirt. He even had this town's top lawyer call me. I was warned to leave him alone. To leave HIM alone. . . ."

Now, she bent her head and her tears dropped beside her glass of Coke. She mopped at them with her paper napkin and talked about how she'd since listened to him speak in a church and before other public gatherings winning over people with his "words of goodness." How, she wanted to know, could he DO that?

I said it sounded to me as if she wanted to punish him. She said that is partly it but partly it is in the hope that at some point the man "will be sorry and concerned about what he's done." He has shattered her belief in decency and redemption. She doesn't want all the guilt, all the bitterness.

I kept mentioning her need for professional counseling. She countered with "Yes, but . . ."

Finally, I told her simply, in my totally unprofessional opinion, she was destroying herself with hatred, a need for revenge. No man, no woman, is immune to trespass. If, indeed, her lover had privately profaned all that he publicly stood for it didn't mean the church was a sham or that decency is forever dead.

My words were lost.

At every public gathering when he mounts the podium there is an attractive young woman seated near the front. Her eyes never leave his face. Forgiveness is an empty word. She can't even forgive herself.

Life has resolved itself into a drama of perverse destruction.

It was a wasted hour. I left depressed and a little sick.

But today, perhaps with prayers of others, two once-vital lives can be restored.

May 10, 1981

"The Day I Stopped Smoking"

Normally, the writing of a column requires 45 to 90 minutes and five to 10 cigarettes.

With a 5 p.m. deadline, I have never dared begin later than 4:10, even when there's no beginning.

I've never begun a column without lighting a cigarette. I've never ended one without lighting a cigarette either, except for an abortive six days many years ago.

I began this column, with a cigarette, at 1:40 p.m. I do not know what time I'll finish. I do know that at this moment . . .

I am stubbing out what my will declares must be The Last Cigarette.

There is little left of it. In 40 years of cigarette addiction I have never left a butt long enough to relight.

Look at all the "I's." Cigarette smoking is full of I's. There will be more as withdrawal symptoms increase because this is going to be an honest chronicle from a dishonest tobacco addict.

Dishonest? Yes. I claim to love life more than cigarettes. To make the claim and to continue smoking is an obvious lie. I have claimed to love others more than myself. It is another lie, since there may be those who self-destruct by emulating me.

An addict, nonetheless, can produce principled arguments without end to defend his or her smoking. An addict can even find his addiction reinforced by no-smoking crusaders.

Usually these people appear to be imperiously self-oriented, themselves considerably flawed in other aspects and totally unaware of their imperfections.

So what brought this decision to stop smoking and to write about it?

Observer staffer Jim Dumbell, a onetime cigarette smoker, suggested it.

At first I was turned off by the stagy, headline-grabbing, stunting aspects of the suggestion.

"You could have a stress test," he said, "a lung-capacity test, a physical in the beginning. This would be a clinical thing, repeated after six months, a year. You could do a heck of a reporting job. Have an idea what this might mean to you and other people?"

That was last week. My cigarette consumption increased from 50 to 60 cigarettes daily as I thought about it and, on Sunday, I wrote about an addict's self-debasement.

Over the years I have tried all the stop-smoking techniques. I've attended clinics for a week at a time. I have used all the gimmicks sold at drugstores. I've cut down gradually and rationed cigarettes to myself, only to end up smoking more and stronger cigarettes.

Once I went "cold turkey" for six days, flew into a rage over nothing and smashed a huge dish on the kitchen wall. I rationed myself to three cigarettes a day for five more weeks and gained 16 pounds. That was my reason to go back to smoking.

The previous sentence will cause a number of cigarette addicts to sigh, light up a cigarette, and coast on idle through the remainder of the column. Fat is a killer. Right? You got to die sometime from something. Right? Oh, yes, and tell them about your grandma who died of emphysema and lung cancer and never smoked anything in her life.

I doubt there is a surefire, universal method to stop smoking. I know smokers who have been "delivered." They woke up one morning after 20 years of enslavement and didn't want to smoke anymore.

If there's a moral giant in this society, it's the man, or woman, who stopped smoking years ago and has never mentioned it to a soul.

Dr. Bill Matthews has told me there is one way practically everybody can stop. "They always quit when I tell them they have cancer," he says. "You're a good bet to find out how easy it is under those circumstances."

Once I went to his office coughing up blood. He asked me if I would stop smoking, regardless of what his tests might show. I said, "Yes." I lied. I didn't have cancer, so, after some hours, I congratulated myself and then seemed to try to smoke myself to death.

Some people, despite Dr. Matthews's experience, keep smoking after discovering they have lung cancer, the logic being that it's too late now to stop.

Recently I visited a friend in a hospital, just emerging from a critical bout with pneumonia, but smoking. My friend's explanation: "It's about the only pleasure I have left. . . .''

Thought processes have been interrupted dozens of times by the cigarette brain signal in almost two hours of writing. It rolls across the consciousness with a steady rhythm.

I guess it is because in 40 years I have never had a thought without a cigarette, never initiated an action as the result of thought without a cigarette.

The stress test and lung-capacity tests are upcoming as soon as Bill Matthews sets them up. I'll tell you about it when and if I can come down off the wall.

January 16, 1979

The Very End

E.H. phoned in a recorded query: "What are the present members of the President's Cabinet at this moment?" I assume E.H. meant to ask "Who" instead of "What" since the latter would call for a subjective judgment we'd rather not make. But, E.H., in the interest of accuracy, at what moment did you place your call?

March 5, 1974

Afterword

Kays Gary is a short intense man with a worry frown on his forehead. He was probably born with gray hair. We met at U.S. military headquarters in Berlin before the wall went up. A few anonymous authorities said that the presence of Kays Gary was the reason the communists put the wall up.

As a columnist, he is one of the finest human interest writers in America. He was always a craftsman, one who solemnly chiselled each phrase in stone. He is a hard-boiled soft touch easily moved by a hard luck story or an injustice.

Mr. Gary is the lord high columnist of lost causes, the St. Jude of Journalism. What he writes would draw red corpuscles from a rock. He is sure that, given time, he can correct the ills of the world. He may be right.

Jim Bishop, 1981